# Studio Shape Up

# STUDIO SHAPE UP

## The Keys to Transforming Your Fitness Studio Into a Thriving Business

### Chelsea Streifeneder

Dear Jeevis
#pilatesaprossico Mark-
Thank you for all your support!!
love
CS

NEW YORK

LONDON • NASHVILLE • MELBOURNE • VANCOUVER

# Studio Shape Up

*The Keys to Transforming Your Fitness Studio Into a Thriving Business*

Published in New York, New York, by Morgan James Publishing. Morgan James is a trademark of Morgan James, LLC. www.MorganJamesPublishing.com

The Morgan James Speakers Group can bring authors to your live event. For more information or to book an event visit The Morgan James Speakers Group at www.TheMorganJamesSpeakersGroup.com.

ISBN 9781642790603 paperback
ISBN 9781642790610 eBook
Library of Congress Control Number: 2018941612

**Cover Design by:**
Rachel Lopez
www.r2cdesign.com

**Interior Design by:**
Christopher Kirk
GFSstudio.com

In an effort to support local communities, raise awareness and funds, Morgan James Publishing donates a percentage of all book sales for the life of each book to Habitat for Humanity Peninsula and Greater Williamsburg.

Get involved today! Visit
www.MorganJamesBuilds.com

*Dedicated to entrepreneurs & teachers who keep moving forward & believe that anything is possible.*

# Table of Contents

———— • ————

# Acknowledgements

———————————  •  ———————————

S *tudio Shape Up* is finally here and I want to take a moment to thank everyone who has helped push me through this incredible journey. Writing this book was a whirlwind, and more rewarding than I ever could have imagined. Thank you to every single person who read, reviewed, supported and contributed to my book. I greatly appreciate all the time you gifted me.

Thanks to: The whole Morgan James Publishing team, for taking a chance on Studio Shape Up and a girl from upstate New York's book proposal. You made this a dream come true.

My wonderful editor, Margot Dougherty, whose valuable guidance helped me through this roller coaster of a ride to shape up the book you now hold in your hands.

My Body Be Well Pilates team. You all are so special and you make the studios what they are today. Without all of you this book and Body Be Well Pilates would not be possible. Every day you encourage our clients and push me to be better. Thank you for your commitment, for your dedication and time, your generosity with each other and with me. I appreciate all of you, each and every day.

To all the Body Be Well Pilates clients, fans and followers, your dedication and love for Pilates and the studios have kept me going for the past decade. We are still moving forward and always learning and growing with you. The enthusiasm and determination each and every one of you have brought inside (and outside) the studios have been the best gifts ever.

To Robin Cherry. Thank you for holding me accountable and being my guide through this long journey. I am so blessed for your advice and help every step of the way and always with a smile and caring words. You are brilliant, insightful and beyond patient. Even when I was stuck, exhausted, and didn't know what to do or where to go, you were there for me one hundred percent of the time.

To Andromeda & Kelli. Without both of you and The Pilates Sports Center I wouldn't have started this journey and lovefest with Pilates. Thank you for pushing me through and still guiding and supporting me over a decade later!

And lastly, to my wonderful family and friends, thank you for all your encouragement and support. Papa, thank you for telling me to always dream big and showing me that with hard work anything is possible. Mom, thank you for raising me to be an independent and strong woman and for always being my biggest fan. To Shannon and Dillon for being a daily source of inspiration and motivation. You both constantly amaze me. Thank you, Oma for being the best grandmother anyone could ask for. To Steven for listening to me type at all hours and reminding me to stop and breathe. And to Missy and Jess for being real and always being there for me. I love you all! Thank you!

# Introduction

———————————————— • ————————————————

Setting up and running a fitness studio can be an exhilarating and exciting proposition, and it also requires a lot of really hard work. Believe me, I know.

I opened, Body Be Well Pilates, a 600 square foot studio in New York's Hudson Valley, over a decade ago. Since then I've tripled the initial studio space three times, opened a second studio, and bought the two buildings the studios are in. I have a lot of friends who are studio owners—yoga, spin, and of course Pilates—some in urban areas, some more remote, and found myself giving them outside-the-box suggestions about how to attract clients, encourage loyalty (a key aspect of this business), and improve profits. Seeing how well certain tips and ideas worked for them inspired me to help others that might have similar issues or things obstructing their paths. I wrote this book to spread the word outside my immediate circle—I want to give you the down-and-dirty of what it's really like to own and run your own fitness studio, how to avoid some common pitfalls and, equally important, how to maximize the rewards of this business model. I want this book to be as beneficial to you as movement and exercise are to your clients.

Owning a business is not for the faint of heart. Beneath the serene atmosphere of a Pilates, yoga, or any other type of fitness studio, lies a chaotic mess of scheduling, payroll, taxes, insurance, building and equipment maintenance, and infinite amounts of other things that add up—who's going to clean the bathrooms, where will the lost and found be? Owning a business is a juggling act. It takes a lot of concentration. And because every studio is different, as is every location, there is no universal code or plan that will work for everyone. The key is to create a studio that specifically addresses the needs and expectations of your clientele and reflects you and your teaching style.

I run a Pilates studio, but I've learned that the challenges I face are comparable to those faced by studio owners in other fitness disciplines as well — yoga, spinning, personal training, and dance. Most of us have chosen this career because we love to teach and help people, but we have to remember that, at the end of the day, we're running a business. And running a business takes, ingenuity, perseverance, fiscal discipline—and guts. Believe me, there were days early on when I wondered if I could keep the doors open. Our clients take vacations, our bills don't, so it's key to have an overall approach that allows for the inevitable ebbs and flows of attendance and income. In the following chapters, I'll give you tools for navigating the rougher times so they don't pull you underwater.

Whether your goal is to open a new business, optimize the studio you have, take your profit up a few notches—or just grow your class following as a teacher, I hope this book will give you the information you need to prosper. I want to share what I've done to create successful studios—I'll let you in on what's worked, and, just as important, what hasn't.

I hope that what I've learned as a student, teacher and studio owner over the years will help you navigate through some roadblocks and create a sound foundation so you can fast forward to a healthy and thriving business.

Let's get started!

# In the Beginning

———————— • ————————

Before you get too deep into this idea of opening a studio or spiffing up the one you already have, let's see if its an undertaking that's the best fit for your personality and skill set. Do you ever wonder if being an employee would actually be more fun than running a studio and taking responsibility for a whole mess of extra necessities, from cleaning the toilets to making sure there's water in the fridge at all times to cleaning up after classes and keeping everyone's egos buoyant and happy?

This test might give you some clues.

## Pop Quiz!

1. Are you prepared to wear 3,045 hats?

2. Are you aware that running your own studio may require 12 to 18 hour days, 7 days a week and/or holidays?

3. Can you handle the physical and emotional aspects of the above workload?

4. Are you ready to put your business first and possibly lower your standard of living until your business is established?

3

5. Are you okay with not getting paid?

6. Can you handle face-to-face confrontation and not-so-happy clients?

7. Are you okay with running back to the studio after finally finishing your 10+ hour shift with shampoo in your hair because one of your teachers forgot and/or lost her key and cannot find the hidden key to get into the studio and the whole class is waiting when you get there?

8. Are you okay asking people for money and letting them know the studio's prices have increased?

9. Are your family, partner, friends and fur babies prepared to support you?

10. Do you have a substantial savings account and are you prepared to use it?

11. Can you multitask—interact with clients, run the front desk, fix overflowing toilets, deal with clients who aren't signed in but are here for class, all at the same time?

12. Can you create new programs, run a business, teach, plan and organize all in one day?

13. Can you be a cheerleader and the bad guy at the same time?

14. Are you committed to running and improving your studio even when you are exhausted beyond belief?

15. Are you good at overcoming obstacles, solving problems and realizing that routine may not be in the next days, weeks or years to come?

*If you answered "YES" to every one of these questions without a moment's hesitation, you have entrepreneurship potential.*

# CHAPTER 1
## Setting Up

├────────────── • ──────────────┤

*"Life is the dancer and you are the dance."*
– Eckhart Tolle

Well there I was. I had my mats all laid out and my Pilates class planned and it was almost time for my 5 p.m. class to begin. But where was everyone? I had just opened my studio, Body Be Well, in a small town in New York's Hudson Valley, and had one reformer, a landline, nothing to process credit cards with, and a whole lot of nervous energy. I had no clue what I was doing.

Then, finally, the door opened and in walked...my mom! Great! My first client is my mother. But wait! Two more ladies followed. And then there were three! I took a deep breath, grabbed my confidence and began the class. It was the start of a whirlwind.

We all have stories about how we began our businesses—in my case it was a scary leap. I was living in Los Angeles, and every time I came back to my family's home in Red Hook I'd head for Poets Walk, a beautiful trail overlooking the Hudson River, with Stella, my Maltese puppy. I wanted to be outside as much as possible. However, winters in New York are not always so nice and when there were more than six inches of snow, Stella would get lost beneath it. I was forced to find other options for fitting in my exercise indoors, none of which I was happy with.

So with my man-of-action father (always ready to go, even if he'd had no sleep and had just come off an all-nighter from his job as a signalman at the railroad) and my talented and creative friend Chris by my side, we started the project of all projects—transforming thousands of square feet into studios with possibilities.

Welcome to studio ownership! Some days you may feel like you still don't know what the heck you're doing (being honest!), but somehow, you're doing it and ten years have passed. If you're anything like me, you'll have daily ups and downs, and stretches where you feel like a manic mess.

As soon as you embark on this path, get ready to be slammed with difficult decisions and unexpected situations—more often than not, you'll have to wing it. The details of your challenges will be unique, but I'm hoping that by passing along my experiences yours will be that much easier to handle. If there's one thing I learned in my studios, it's that there isn't a single recipe for studio success, just as there isn't a one-size-fits-all workout for our clients. The details of your challenges will be unique, but I'm hoping my experiences can help make yours easier to handle.

The two key elements of business ownership are getting clients through the door and creating experiences that will bring them back. Client loyalty is key. Client loyalty cannot be bought. It must be earned, and not just once, but every day of the studio owner-client relationship. Never take it for granted. I am grateful that I still have a large percentage of the first bunch of bodies that walked through my doors.

A happy client is one who will bring you business again and again and cut down on your need to spend time and effort attracting new business. Happy clients will likely refer their friends to you.

So how can we make our first students committed and forever students, or our "founders," as Elaine Economou, co-owner and teacher at Move Wellness, a Pilates studio in Michigan, likes to call her first 20 clients.

You may have heard the old business saying, "It costs less to keep clients than to get new ones." So when looking for founders, or "lifers" as we call them, be consistent. Say please and thank you, make their problems your problems and fix them.

To get yourself focused on exactly what services you're providing, brainstorm short, bold descriptions and settle on one that could grab a new client (or investor) before the elevator hits the 10th floor. The proverbial elevator pitch. How can we tell people what we do quickly and effectively without losing them, and how can we get them intrigued in our studio while standing in the grocery line, grabbing a coffee or at the post office? Can you tell people what you do in four words or less?

"Resistance training with springs," is how pioneer instructor, Alycea Ungaro, of Manhattan's Real Pilates, describes Pilates.

Think about how you'd like to present Pilates (or yoga, or whatever regimen it is that you offer) to your clients and develop your own elevator speech. Invest in business cards that you are proud of, that reflect you and your brand. Along with contact info and your logo (yes, you should have a logo), consider including a photo of your snazzy self. Be sure to give your cards out when you bump into people new and old. Always be ready to promote and scream about your business from the rooftops. Don't be shy. Telling people face-to-face, in my opinion, is the best way to get clients and to promote yourself and your studio. And the best part is…. it's FREE!

As I said earlier, getting people through our doors is a top priority if we want our business to thrive, and it's something we have to work on continuously. The time to promote is not when you have run out of clients.

So after you've found your perfect location and studio space, there are lots of things that need to happen. Maybe you've seen that quote (or t-shirt) by illustrator Lori Hetteen: "I don't have ducks. Or rows. I have squirrels at a rave." That pretty much describes how starting up and running a business can be. Below is a checklist to complete before opening your doors—Make sure you have more ducks than squirrels!

Studio Start Up Checklist:

❑ Find an amazing lawyer! They will help you register your business name (making sure it isn't already taken by someone else), set up your legal structure (so you'll know how much you'll likely pay in taxes, what kind of personal liability insurance you'll need, and what type of corporation you should establish your business as). Your lawyer will also set up your business structure (sole proprietorship, partnership, or corporation, for example) and get your employer identification number (EIN), which you'll need for your taxes.

❑ Find a bank that will work with you and answer any questions you might have. Make sure they have pleasant tellers (you'll be seeing these people on a daily/ weekly basis) and then open your business account.

❑ Choose a domain name—ideally the same name as your studio. If that domain name is taken, try adding your city or another qualifier to make it unique: Patsy Pilates Adirondacks, for example. Buy your domain name and create a professional website—or hire someone to do it for you. Your website will be the front door of your business, so don't skimp on this. If you're not tech-minded, be sure to have someone you can rely on to keep the site current and operational.

❑ Design a logo that represents you and your brand—or, again, hire a pro to do it for you.

❑ If you're planning on having employees, make sure they've filled out I-9 and W-4 forms. If you're planning on having independent contractors (your lawyer will help you determine the difference between employees and independent contractors), make sure you have legal forms for them to sign with an agreement between you, them and the studio.

❑ Create a handbook outlining everything from dress code to payroll and how we take payment. You'll give a copy to all teachers and staff.

❑ Determine your class schedule, when you will be open, how much you will charge for classes, and what systems you will use to make a flawless experience for clients and staff. Will you use an online sign up platform or go old school and keep class cards to start?

❑ Buy your insurance and make sure you're protected as much as you can be against personal injury, fire, flood, etc.

❑ Draw up liability waivers for students to sign. It's also a good idea to have health history forms which they can fill out. This info will be useful to you when tailoring classes and sessions to their needs. Electronic versions will make everyone's lives easier.

❑ Get your sign up. But before you do, check with your town/city ordinances to be sure the sign meets local standards. Check with your landlord to make sure it meets their criteria as well.

❑ Figure out who you're gonna call if: your heat stops working in the middle of winter, the toilet overflows, a pipe bursts, you have a leak in the roof, or a window shatters. Is our landlord responsible for some or all of these or are you the landlord? Who will clean the studio and maintain your equipment? Make sure you have a list of reliable go-to people.

❑ Monthly studio supplies. Will you have these automatically delivered or will your grandmother buy your toilet paper, soap and paper towels for you with her coupon shopping addiction? Do you have a water cooler? Make sure you have plans to keep all these essentials fully stocked in the most cost-effective way possible.

❑ Marketing materials. Have a hefty supply with you and at the studio to hand out and inform people about you, your business and what you do.

## CHAPTER 2
# You've Got Students. Now What?

├────────────────── • ──────────────────┤

*"It's the supreme art of the teacher to awaken joy in
creative expression and knowledge."*
— Albert Einstein

So you've assembled a small staff (or are going it alone for
now), dealt with all the studio start-up needs, and have a stack
of health history forms and liability waivers your clients can sign
before they get started. Now what?

As trainers, we've become skilled educators and motivators
who inspire healthy bodies and lifestyles. We want all our classes
and sessions to flow from one movement to the next, and to make
everyone feel better and more energized by the end. But what about
the business side? How do we get clients to buy and commit—it's
in their best interest, and ours, to come to the studio at least once a
week. Here are some ways to encourage them to do so.

### ~ Welcome Packs ~

Let's be honest. A first session with a trainer is like a first date—
for the client and for the trainer. As soon as our new "date" walks
into the studio, we may be a little nervous; we're trying our best to

impress them so they'll want to see us again. Hopefully the session goes well, they pay (sometimes even before the session) and we wait to see if they come back.

After the first session, we learn a lot. Sometimes we realize that this person is or is not the client for us. Or perhaps we're not the perfect trainer for them. For example if the newbie tells you that they hate training with a man and you're, well, a man, then that might not be a good match. Or, if halfway through the session your newbie announces that they forgot to mention on their health history form that they just had a lumpectomy, and you haven't had any training in this, that's not so good either. In this case, we can hopefully set them up with another trainer in the studio who is equipped to deal with medical issues. This also goes for group classes. The teacher or the group might not be the right fit for a specific client.

Hopefully you won't take offense if the client prefers another trainer. It's just a chemistry thing. What's important is that the client is happy and keeps coming back to your studio. But if they leave, that's okay, too! They weren't meant to be there. Sometimes it takes many, many first dates to find those perfect clients you'll want regular standing appointments with every week.

After we've made a good first impression, what can we do to go above and beyond our clients' expectations to show them how much we appreciate them and–what we're all about? I suggest a Welcome Pack—a note sent to the client's home along with a few goodies to show your appreciation.

Invest in branded and/or personal stationery (I have postcards with the studio logo as well as letterhead with the studio's name) so you can mail a handwritten postcard after their first session:

# OBLONG BOOKS & MUSIC

Montgomery Row          Rhinebeck
(845) 876-0500
Shop 24/7 at oblongbooks.com

Returns allowed w/in 14 days w/ receipt.

```
   136579 Reg 3 6:39 pm 02/16/19
S STUDIO SHAPE UP T   1 @ 17.95    17.95
SUBTOTAL                           17.95
SALES TAX - 8.125%                  1.46
TOTAL                              19.41
AMERICAN EXPRESS PAYMENT           19.41
Account# XXXXXXXXXXX4281  Exp Date 0222
Authorization# 494842
```

I agree to pay the above total amount
according to the card issuer agreement.

UPCOMING EVENTS:
1/27 Kids' Event: Nancy Furstinger
2/2 Andrew Delbanco @ Starr Library
2/5 Ted Fox SHOWTIME AT THE APOLLO
2/9 Michael Crupain WHAT TO EAT WHEN

13657 Reg 3 6:35 pm 02/16/19
S STUDIO SHAPE UP T   1 @ 17.35   17.95
SUBTOTAL                            17.95
SALES TAX - 8.125%                   1.46
TOTAL                               19.41
AMERICAN EXPRESS PAYMENT            19.41
Account# XXXXXXXXXXX4281   Exp Date 0222
Authorization# 494842

I agree to pay the above total amount
according to the card issuer agreement

UPCOMING EVENTS:
1/27 Kids' Event: Nancy Furstinger
2/2 Andrew Delbanco @ Starr Library
2/5 Ted Fox SHOWTIME AT THE APOLLO
2/9 Michael Ohpatn WHAT TO EAT WHEN

Welcome to (Name of Your Business)!

We loved having you at our studio and hope you enjoyed your first session. Please don't hesitate to reach out with questions or concerns—we're here for you! Looking forward to seeing you again soon.

Be Well,

(Your Name) & the (Name of Your Business) Team

Or, if you want to do something a little more in depth:

Dear (Name of Client)

I wanted to personally welcome you to (Name of Your Business), and thank you for walking through our doors. All of us at (Name of Your Business) do our best to ensure that we're more than just a place to work out, and that means treating our clients as friends. Our goal isn't just to increase your strength, but also to make sure that you're enjoying the experience along the way.

If you ever have any questions, comments or concerns, please don't hesitate to contact me or any of our knowledgeable team members. Remember, we're always here to help.

Until next time,

(Your Name)

In addition to the initial postcard, we gift newbies a welcome letter in a goody bag—our Welcome Pack. We throw in some gifts and product samples in addition to incentive coupons. You can pick one or two things (see our sample list below) that will be affordable and tie into your fitness business. It's always fun to switch things around every quarter. People really appreciate our notes and goody bags.

When a new business opens in town, it's a perfect opportunity to go in and introduce yourself to the owners. Making yourself and your business an integral part of your neighborhood is a great way to build community goodwill. You may find that local businesses are a good source of goodies for the Welcome Packs—the businesses get exposure to your clients, your clients get a treat, and you get happy clients as a result. Win-win-win.

On the next page is a sample welcome letter. You can use it as a template to create one that fits your studio and clientele.

•

Here are some of the sample coupons that are popular with our clients:

- ✓ Present this coupon to receive 25% off one retail item at our boutique. Check out our athleisure wear and other fitness swag that you soon won't be able to live without!

- ✓ Present this coupon to receive 50% off your first "Workout & Takeout" event. Come work out, then redeem the coupon to join the rest of the class with a healthy meal from a local restaurant, or take it home with you.

- ✓ Present this coupon to receive your first three pairs of grip socks for $35. These socks will not only keep your feet clean and warm, but also help you grip the equipment and floor to keep you safe. Added perk: They look great!

Welcome to (Name of Your Business).

We are so excited that you joined us for your 1st session at our studio. Get ready for a workout and learning experience that will change your body! There are so many exciting, challenging and transformational experiences waiting for you.

Your 1st session gave you a little preview about us and what our studio is about. After a few more sessions, you'll have a more complete picture of what the workouts are like and how you'll benefit in the weeks to come.

If you are new to fitness, some exercises may be a little different than you expected, so please feel free to ask us any questions or share your preferences so we can provide you with the best possible experience.

So now what?

Reserve Your Spots: Schedule your class(es) or session(s) that will fit into your lifestyle and daily schedule. Be consistent and realistic when making your appointments.

Stay Focused: When you are here, give those 50 minutes your full 100% attention. Your "me time" here is just as important as any other appointment, so don't cancel on yourself.

Do Your Homework: The more moving outside the studio the better your results in the studio will be. You will reach your goals a lot faster and your body—and trainer—will thank you!

Try it All: Try different classes, different equipment and different trainers. Change is a good thing for your brain and body.

Please test out the samples in your gift bag and feel free to use the new client specials attached to this letter. Enjoy, and we look forward to seeing you at the studio.

Be Well,

(Name of Owner)

✓ Present this coupon to receive $15 off a massage or facial with our in-house masseuse/aesthetician. *(Studio owners: If you work with a local spa, facialists or body workers, you might be able to coordinate a coupon with them.)*

✓ Present this coupon at (name of local juice bar or coffee shop) to receive a small beverage on the house.

Along with the coupons, some of the goodies we like to include in our Welcome Packs are:

✓ Sample of a skincare product or a package of bath salts from either a local business or a company whose products we sell at our fitness boutique. (If you sell retail, it's always a good idea to promote the products you sell. You can give out a sample and if your clients love it, which of course they will, they'll come back and buy full-size products at full price.)

✓ A healthy energy bar, so clients don't get hangry.

✓ A postcard promoting online workouts (your own or another program you endorse and think they'll like). We want our clients to realize that moving outside the studio will make their time inside the studio even more productive.

✓ We have a local tea maker (shout out to Harney & Sons!) and work with them to pick appropriate teas that complement pre- and post-workout times. We use their "Athletea" line with a tea that comes in three flavors and we wrap a few in a bag, and give them out.

✓ A sticker or temporary tattoo with your logo and/or tagline on it.

Of course there are many other options, so think about what will resonate with your clients, be creative, and have fun! Local businesses are usually more than willing to help out—it's as good for their bottom line and visibility as it is for yours.

# CHAPTER 3

# Hiring, Training &
# Retaining Your Team

⊢─────────── • ───────────⊣

*"You can employ men and hire hands to work for you,
but you will have to win their hearts to have them
work with you."*
— William J.H. Boetcker, author and motivational speaker

S ome of you may prefer to run a one-person studio without both-ering with the personalities and stresses of a staff. My good friend, April Walker, owner of Lifetree Pilates Studio in Valatie, NY wouldn't want it any other way.

"My business model has always been to work alone in my own studio," she says. "I have always referred to myself as a one-woman show. I know that I tend to be a bit meticulous about certain things and I prefer to work solo so I can keep my standards high. I work long hours, I clean the bathroom, I shovel the snow, and I do all the things to keep my studio running smoothly. Sometimes it's draining, but mostly rewarding, both personally and financially. I work for myself, I am my own boss, and when something doesn't go exactly as planned, I fix it!"

April has some great advice for anyone thinking about doing it alone: "Know before you start what you want to accomplish with your business endeavor. Create goals, meet them and create more goals…always strive to do better. Be compassionate and kind. Pilates is bodywork and has a very healing element to it, and with that comes a tremendous amount of responsibility. People will trust you to know how to help them; they will look to you for knowledge and support. Do your work so you are able to rise to the challenge. My Pilates teacher taught me not to be afraid to say that you don't know something, but always, always, go and do the research, so that you will know the next time you see your client. (Thanks Chelsea!!!)"

Although I started out on my own (I didn't know how else to do it), I always knew I wanted to grow my business, and for that I'd need a staff—teachers as well as folks to handle the stuff I wasn't good at/interested in, like the retail boutique, cleaning, and other studio duties.

## ~ *Employee or Independent Contractor?* ~

Call them whatever you want…your squad, your tribe, your homies, or your team. You know how important your staff is to your business. Recognizing them is a super important part of retaining the best of the best and recruiting new team members when needed.

Here's a BIG controversy in the fitness industry—with probably enough debate for an entire book: Independent Contractor vs. Employee. How do you distinguish one from the other and choose which is best for your business?

This is a topic incessantly debated, but one thing is certain: Not knowing the difference between can be detrimental to your business. In my opinion hiring independent contractors in the startup phase may be the best option. However, as your business grows, it might be in your best interest to switch everyone over to employee status.

An independent contractor determines on their own where they work and when they work and they make their own hours. Unless you include a clause negating it in their contract, they have the right to refuse teaching on your studio's class schedule. Independent contractors have to pay their own self-employment taxes and will usually work at more than one location. The can change fees, have their own brand, and promote themselves without mentioning your business or space if they so choose.

An employee, on the other hand, can be required to teach a certain amount of hours a week, or to teach certain classes on the studio's schedule. Specific trainings might be mandatory for them to attend or have completed, wardrobe and/or uniform codes can be enforced, and employees can be required to attend promotional events or parties at your studio. They can also be required to reach out to clients that have been MIA from the studio, and cover classes and sessions when another teacher is away or sick.

In my opinion, it's best to make everyone who works for you an employee at the studio. Yes, there might be more paperwork and leadership duties, but I believe it helps keep your business professional, real and legal. Studio owners or not, teachers and trainers are educators. What we do isn't a hobby or just something fun we dabble in on the weekends.

I've given you a brief description of the difference between an employee and independent contractor, but why not get clarification straight from the horse's mouth! Below are the definitions from the IRS website. Being a government document, it's not a super-fun read, but when you're hiring, decide whether you want employees, independent contractors, or a combination of the two.

It's a fine line between the two, but your choice will affect your bottom line and your taxes, so it's important to learn the distinction. If the IRS ever comes knocking, you'll want to be able to back up your interpretation. Here's what they have to say:

*It's critical that business owners correctly determine whether the individuals providing services are employees or independent contractors.*

*Generally, you must withhold income taxes, withhold and pay Social Security and Medicare taxes, and pay unemployment tax on wages paid to an employee. You do not generally have to withhold or pay any taxes on payments to independent contractors.*

*Select the Scenario that Applies to You:*

- I am an independent contractor or in business for myself.

  *If you are a business owner or contractor who provides services to other businesses, then you are generally considered self-employed.*

- I hire or contract with individuals to provide services to my business.

  *If you are a business owner hiring or contracting with other individuals to provide services, you must determine whether the individuals providing services are employees or independent contractors.*

*How do you determine whether the individuals providing services are employees or independent contractors?*

*Before you can determine how to treat payments you make for services, you must first know the business relationship that exists between you and the person performing the services. The person performing the services may be –*

- An independent contractor.
- An employee (common-law employee).

Common Law Rules:

*Facts that provide evidence of the degree of control and independence fall into three categories:*

- Behavioral: *Does the company control or have the right to control what the worker does and how the worker does his or her job?*

- Financial: *Are the business aspects of the worker's job controlled by the payer? (These include things like how worker is paid, whether expenses are reimbursed, who provides tools/supplies, etc.)*
- Type of Relationship: *Are there written contracts or employee type benefits (i.e. pension plan, insurance, vacation pay, etc.)? Will the relationship continue and is the work performed a key aspect of the business?*

*Businesses must weigh all these factors when determining whether a worker is an employee or independent contractor. Some factors may indicate that the worker is an employee, while other factors indicate that the worker is an independent contractor. There is no "magic" or set number of factors that "makes" the worker an employee or an independent contractor, and no one factor stands alone in making this determination. Also, factors, which are relevant in one situation, may not be relevant in another.*

*The keys are to look at the entire relationship, consider the degree or extent of the right to direct and control, and finally, to document each of the factors used in coming up with the determination.*

*The Internal Revenue Service reminds small businesses of the importance of understanding and correctly applying the rules for classifying a worker as an employee or an independent contractor. For federal employment tax purposes, a business must examine the relationship between it and the worker. The IRS Small Business and Self-Employed Tax Center on the IRS website offers helpful resources.*

*Worker classification is important because it determines if an employer must withhold income taxes and pay Social Security, Medicare taxes and unemployment tax on wages paid to an employee. Businesses normally do not have to withhold or pay any taxes on payments to independent contractors. The earnings of a person working as an independent contractor are subject to self-employment tax.*

*The general rule is that an individual is an independent contractor if the payer has the right to control or direct only the result of the work, not what will be done and how it will be done. Small businesses should consider all evidence of the degree of control and independence in the employer/worker relationship. Whether a worker is an independent contractor or employee depends on the facts in each situation.*

Help with Deciding

*To better determine how to properly classify a worker, consider these three categories – Behavioral Control, Financial Control and Relationship of the Parties.*

Behavioral Control: *A worker is an employee when the business has the right to direct and control the work performed by the worker, even if that right is not exercised. Behavioral control categories are:*

- *Type of instructions given, such as when and where to work, what tools to use or where to purchase supplies and services. Receiving the types of instructions in these examples may indicate a worker is an employee.*

- *Degree of instruction, more detailed instructions may indicate that the worker is an employee. Less detailed instructions reflect less control, indicating that the worker is more likely an independent contractor.*

- *Evaluation systems to measure the details of how the work is done points to an employee. Evaluation systems measuring just the end result point to either an independent contractor or an employee.*

- *Training a worker on how to do the job — or periodic or on-going training about procedures and methods —*

*is strong evidence that the worker is an employee. Independent contractors ordinarily use their own methods.*

Financial Control: *Does the business have a right to direct or control the financial and business aspects of the worker's job? Consider:*

- *Significant investment in the equipment the worker uses in working for someone else.*

- *Unreimbursed expenses, independent contractors are more likely to incur unreimbursed expenses than employees.*

- *Opportunity for profit or loss is often an indicator of an independent contractor.*

- *Services available to the market. Independent contractors are generally free to seek out business opportunities.*

- *Method of payment. An employee is generally guaranteed a regular wage amount for an hourly, weekly, or other period of time even when supplemented by a commission. However, independent contractors are most often paid for the job by a flat fee.*

Relationship: *The type of relationship depends upon how the worker and business perceive their interaction with one another. This includes:*

1. *Written contracts, which describe the relationship, the parties intend to create. Although a contract stating the worker is an employee or an independent contractor is not sufficient to determine the worker's status.*

2. *Benefits. Businesses providing employee-type benefits, such as insurance, a pension plan, vacation pay or sick pay have employees. Businesses generally do not grant these benefits to independent contractors.*

3. *The permanency of the relationship is important. An expectation that the relationship will continue indefinitely, rather than for a specific project or period, is generally seen as evidence that the intent was to create an employer-employee relationship.*

4. *Services provided which is a key activity of the business. The extent to which services performed by the worker is seen as a key aspect of the regular business of the company.*

Deciding how you want to categorize the teachers and support staff working for you is important for financial reasons, but also because it will impact the investment and enthusiasm your workers have for you and the studio. Nobody is ever going to treat your business with the same singleness of vision and passion as you—it isn't theirs. Their name isn't on the mortgage(s) or lease(s) or equipment loan documents. However, your name is on their paycheck and/or rental agreement if they are independent and just using your space. If you choose your staff carefully you'll find teachers fully dedicated to their clients and to you.

"One of my greatest *aha* moments," says Real Pilates Alycea Ungaro, "was recognizing that I don't have to do it alone and that I truly love working in a team. Part two was building that team."

So how do we do go from being a solo act to leading a fantastic crew?

Hiring a new team member for your studio is an exciting, stressful and scary time. It can feel intimidating, as the risks are high. Every team member you add to the mix has an important impact on client retention and your studio's perception. So:

## ~ *Have Patience* ~

This has been and is still a work in progress for me. The right people are out there, but finding them is not always easy, especially when you needed help last month. Hiring employees because you *have* to fill an open position is a recipe for disaster. In fact, having *no one* is better than hiring someone who doesn't accurately represent your studio brand and culture. Make and take the time to sit down with the candidate, take one of their classes if they're teaching or ask for a one-on-one session. Whether you're planning on doing it all alone, having a small or huge team, working with family, just hang in there and breathe until you find the right person.

I admire Pilates Methodology's founder Rachael Lieck Bryce's patience and process. When hiring new teachers for her Dallas, TX studio, she asks people on her team to lead at least one of the three interviews, and has her studio manager sit in on two of the three. It always helps to have second opinions.

"First and foremost," Rachael says, "you can't get it right 100% of the time. I have certainly struck out, but I keep striking out to a minimum through a three-part hiring process. The qualities I look for the most in someone are: Can they give and receive feedback and can they be a team player who is thoughtful and thinks outside of themselves? One of my questions on part two of the process is: How will you handle hard feedback when it is given? The best answer to date was, 'I would first self reflect.' I almost didn't do part three of the interview; I knew she would be hired! I have a list of non-negotiables, and it is easy to see, by how people respond to that list, whether or not they would be a good fit. I also talk openly about the fact that it doesn't just have to work for me; it also has to work for them.

## ~ *Always Be On the Lookout* ~

Even when you're fully staffed, you should be thinking about hiring new team members. Keep an open mind, because you never know where or when you might find your perfect next hire.

A new local restaurant opened near my studio at a time when I was in need of some extra hands. It turned out the restaurant owner wasn't able to give his employees as many hours as they wanted, so I asked if it would be okay if I interviewed a couple of them. I was able to give the workers some extra hours at the studio, which allowed them to continue at the restaurant. We all benefited.

When you constantly keep an eye out for potential team members for your studios, you won't be pressured to hire a mediocre instructor, ho-hum front desk help or anyone else because you're desperate. Instead, you'll fill your next open position with an awesome candidate you actually *want*.

## ~ Be Black and White About the Qualities You Seek ~

It all starts with the job description. The initial job description provides you, as a studio owner, with the opportunity to define the type of team member you want to hire. You won't find your next perfect hire without clearly defining the position and the type of person you're looking for.

Really take the time and figure out what you need and want. Do you value experience, education, and professionalism? Are you focused on hiring an employee who is friendly and outgoing? Or is it more important to you to find someone who is exceptionally organized?

Make a list of the specific qualities you're looking for and accept nothing less than the best.

## ~ Ask the Right Questions ~

Once you've determined which qualities you want for your next rock-star employee, develop interview questions to help you determine if an applicant has those qualities. Be specific. Generic questions won't provide the insight you need to make an informed hiring decision.

Also be aware of your time and your staff's time about face-to-face interviews. You don't need to interview every single applicant in person. Pick up the phone and set up an interview to help weed through the riffraff. Prepare a few basic questions and make sure the person on the other end has enough experience and expertise to meet your standards.

"Finding great help is a challenge!" says Karen Ellis, owner/curator of Pilates Nerd®. "I've learned the most from this piece of the business so far. There are people who are far better at certain things than me and I thank goodness for that. I'm a creative type, not necessarily a linear thinker. Also, great help isn't motivated by money alone. Doing a great job, period, drives amazing employees. I believe this is true with all successful businesses. I can't employ people who don't share our vision, so sometimes we get swamped because we are short-staffed, which leads to my wanting more balance in my life. See how the getting good help is so important?"

## ~ Don't Underestimate Team Spirit ~

You could hire the world's best instructor or the world's best front desk employee, but if they can't work with your team, they won't last. Or worse, they'll create problems in your current team's dynamic. The last thing you want is a hostile or stressful work environment for your current team. It's bad for your employees and your studio's clients—and for you!

During their interview, ask questions that focus on working with a team. This will help to determine if your candidate is a team player.

## ~ Hire Certified Trainers ~

This is key and you should pride yourself on having top-notch teachers. If you don't offer a training program of your own, then establish a relationship with a reputable training program that will help certify teachers for you. You'll gain access to new instructors who have the skills and education that will enhance your studio's reputation.

Make sure that the trainers you're interviewing haven't gone through weekend warrior programs and after a weekend of training (maybe 16 hours max) think they're ready to teach and train. Watch out for online programs as well. Some programs allow anyone to print out their certificates after a few hours online and a short test. This way of "training" is not beneficial to anyone.

Make sure your trainers are fully certified, with a minimum of a 450-hour program that was hands-on and completed in a studio. They must be interested in continuous learning and be able to keep clients safe while training them.

## ~ *Test Out the Water* ~

After you go through the interview and possible class or session, give your new hires a trial period. We give a three-month try-out period so we can see if the relationship will grow and move forward or if some things need to change or end. It may be pretty obvious within the first few weeks if your hire will work out, and this period also gives you time to see their potential and ability as well as the dynamic they create with students and other studio team members. Get feedback from your existing employees.

## ~ *Five-Star Work Environment* ~

Who doesn't like five stars or first class? Create a work environment that rewards team members who go the extra mile. Offer staff incentives, such as discounted merchandise and classes, continuing education opportunities, and monthly employee challenges rewarded with $$ or gift cards. Build strategies and practices to make your current team members happy.

Rachael Lieck Bryce gives gift cards to the trainer who subs the most classes in a year and to the teacher with the highest overall retention rate. This keeps her instructors constantly motivated.

Building and managing a great studio team doesn't stop when a new position is filled. It takes work and dedication to move forward, and keep in mind that not everyone will necessarily move forward with you. Be flexible with your plans and ready for change, and stay open to creative ways to solve different challenges. Believe me, they'll be presented to you all the time.

## ~ Show Your Team You Care ~

You know who your top employees are—they're the ones who manage their weekly schedule with ease and get along well with their coworkers. They're the ones who make your job as a manager or owner easier than you could have imagined possible, and they're the ones who deserve your recognition and appreciation. Find a time that's right to show your employees that you care.

I mentioned a few ideas in the Five-Star Work Environment section, but this is such an important aspect of running a studio, I want to amplify the idea. Think of creative ways to show your team your appreciation and help them succeed in their professional and personal lives as well.

For example, write a "love letter" to your staff, individually or as a group. Write something about your commitment to your business and your goals—what you believe is possible with them by your side. Be genuine and authentic and give specific praise. Below is a letter I wrote after one of our holiday parties, right around the New Year.

To My Fabulous and Amazing Team!

First off, I would like to thank you all so much for last night and making our holiday party extra fun and special. It really means a lot to me that you could be there! Your gifts to me were all extra-thoughtful and I appreciate them all very much! Thank you.

I know we don't have much time together where we aren't rushing through our daily lives and teaching, and sometimes it's nice to just take a break and breathe with each other. Sitting back last night and watching all of you, I realized that there is so much that you give to each other and learn from each other and it is of tremendous importance to me that Body Be Well Pilates always has this. There is a reason each of you is at the studios. Thank you for your generosity with each other and with me.

I appreciate every single one of you and I want you all to know that everything you do for the company, Stella (my Maltese), and our team is noticed. You are all a huge piece to this "puzzle," and I appreciate your dedication and the hard work you all do inside and outside of our studios.

Your positive energy in the studios and your positive Pilates approach to your work inspires everyone around you. I look forward to a long and rewarding relationship with each and every one of you. Last year we saw a tremendous growth in our studios and I credit this growth to you. It's because of your sheer dedication and motivation that the company has grown and expanded the way it has.

I am so happy to have you all and excited to see what the future will bring all of us. I am encouraged, inspired and believe in all of you and can't wait to move forward!

Love Always,

Chelsea

## ~ *Team Meetings* ~

Just the thought of team meetings used to make everyone at my studios roll their eyes. I could see they were creating excuses to be busy on that day, just at that time. I even had one girl who made her annual doctor's appointment coincide so she wouldn't have to come and listen to me bitch and complain. All I wanted was everyone to be on the same page!

As Alycea Ungaro of Real Pilates says, "I approach most difficulties in business the same way I approach a client with physical challenges: Identify the limitations and build on whatever is actually available."

Well, the reaction to team meetings was a problem, so I decided to do things differently. Instead of a meeting in the studio, I have a fun "date" (aka meeting) once or twice a year with a non-Pilates activity and food (since everything is better with food in my opinion) and also take each employee out once a year for a one-on-one date—they get to pick where we meet. During the one-on-ones, I tell them to bring some new ideas, issues and things that are bothering them, and we go from there.

During the group events, I quickly go over anything that needs to be talked about, including any upcoming new programs or changes. Later in the week, I send out emails going over everything we spoke about. I also let everyone bring a friend to the event to make it that much more inviting.

Some of our group meeting activities include:
- Paddle Boarding and a Picnic
- Zip Lining and a Picnic
- Bowling
- Rail-Bike Tour and Lunch
- Indoor Rock Climbing

- Hiking and Brunch
- Show and Dinner

## ~ *When It Just Doesn't Work Out* ~

After almost five years of teaching, training and then employing one particular teacher, after many lunch meetings, walks, and cups of coffee, it was time for her to go. She showed up to classes on time, was always present and polite, but there was something missing. She couldn't hold on to clients and people didn't want to take classes with her. When I tried to coach her along with some sample scripts of ways to speak to her classes and clients and with positive feedback she wasn't open to any suggestions. I gave her books, sent her to some workshops, and talked and talked to her about what we could do. Finally, the absence of clients and her attitude were so bad that I felt like I was walking on eggshells in my own studio.

I thought the relationship had ended smoothly, but before I knew it, I was being served legal papers and I had a lawsuit on my hands. After a couple of phone calls to my lawyer, and a letter to her lawyer, everything was dropped, but I will never forget the time, tears, aggravation and money I spent.

My lesson was that I should have let her go a long time before I did. So listen to your gut and know that it's okay to fire people. It didn't hurt my business one bit; if anything it grew even more because some "lost" people returned when she was gone, the rest of my team was happier, and I could breathe and walk in my space again.

Is there a teacher who is out of sync with your studio's awesomeness? Is that one pain-in-the-booty, negative, competitive or entitled teacher who makes nothing but trouble for you still in front of your students? Do what needs to be done. Clean house.

Your studio is serving the clients, not drama-queens or divas. Get over the fear of their anger and what they'll say about you online and just do it already. Your clients, your teachers, and you, deserve much better.

## ~ *Working with Family* ~

Sometimes conversations with my mother start with, "Now don't yell at me Chelsea!" I remember sitting in my parents' sun porch one afternoon with my sister, Shannon, and Mom and having them both ask if I thought they could do "it"? The "it" was teach Pilates. At first I didn't think they were serious, but after a few more minutes of conversation I realized they weren't kidding. They wanted to come work for me.

Fast-forward a couple years: my sister and mom are both teachers and my sister also manages the studios. They are the first ones I turn to when I need help with something.

Working with family can be a *real* challenge, both for the family members and non-family members on staff—and for you as the owner. There have been many days in (and out of) the studio when my sister has threatened to quit and kill me, and sometimes the yelling matches between my mother and I can be heard in China. But at the end of the day, I know I can trust them implicitly and that they have my back.

Family members are not automatically the best people for the job, but, disagreements aside, overall they may be the people you enjoy being around the most. If you decide to go this route, tread with caution, communicate openly, make expectations clear, and be just as fair with your family as you are with your staff. Not all people can say that they love their work team, but I can honestly say that I love everyone on mine, blood relatives included!

# CHAPTER 4

# Memberships & Packages That Make Profits, Not Problems

---•---

*It's not what happens, it's how you handle it.*

Memberships can be beneficial! Through trial and error I finally have a membership program that produces both studio profits and satisfied customers. Here is a story that I refer to over and over again when other business owners ask about memberships.

At an annual Pilates conference in Denver, Colorado another Pilates studio owner tracked me down to discuss membership programs. She follows me on social media and had read something I'd written about a $395 monthly membership available at my studio and wanted to know if such an "expensive" program was working.

She said that while she charged $34 for one group equipment class, she had started offering a monthly membership of $69 for unlimited group classes to compete with a new Barre studio that had opened down the block. Of course, everyone signed up for the unlimited membership—it was just over twice as much as two single classes. How could she expect them to do anything else?

She had a Pilates studio with a room only big enough to fit five Reformers. The unworkability of the arrangement had two things going against her. First, since the $69 membership was unlimited, some clients were signing up for three classes a day. If someone comes once a day, five days a week they are paying $3.45 per class. This doesn't include the cost of the equipment, wear and tear, the limited number of students per class, and payment to the teachers. Second, because she didn't have a cancellation policy, they weren't showing up…. sometimes for all three classes! Clearly, this was unsustainable. Given the cost of her overhead, she was losing money on each class.

At Body Be Well, we offer a Core Membership with three different time frames: 12-month, 3-month and 1-month. If a client signs up for a year, they will pay less than a client who signs a contract for a month. (I've found if you give too many options the clients, employees, teachers and myself all get confused.) I don't use the word "unlimited."

Each level of membership is good for one class a day and a max of seven classes a week. If a client would like to take more than one class a day, they can get a discounted rate of $20 per class instead of the usual $30 (as of this writing). If they would rather take two of their seven classes in one day and skip a day, that's also allowed. If they late-cancel or don't show up, they understand that we have their credit card on file and they will be charged $20 per class unless we can fill their spot with someone on the waitlist. Alternatively, they can gift their spot to a friend who comes in their place. We don't allow clients to rollover their membership, meaning if they only come once or twice in a month, they can't apply their unused classes to the next month. In other words: Use 'em or lose 'em.

We understand that sometimes a medical emergency, an accident or an illness prevents a client from getting to the studio. We handle these situations on a case-by-case basis and, when warranted, will pause the membership until things have returned to normal.

At my studios, I offer discounted bundled classes as an option: three private lessons or three group classes for less than a client would pay on a class-by-class basis. For some, this is a way to get a foot in the door without requiring a major outlay or commitment.

When creating a membership for your studio, it's important to remember the following:

Rule 1: Don't compete with non-competitors. A Barre class is not a Pilates class and a Pilates class is not a TRX or spin class. The economics are completely different; so don't base your prices on what another studio's offering.

Rule 2: Price yourself competitively, but make sure you can earn enough to stay in business—or soon you won't be. Depending on your demographic (or shoe fetish) your bills, rent, and equipment costs are going to vary. Be sure you know them.

Rule 3: Keep it simple. Don't offer too many package options or you'll confuse your clients, your teachers and even yourself.

Rule 4: Cover your costs. Make sure you can pay your overhead and your teachers and staff, assuming there are other folks on the payroll, with your membership rates. Also, make sure there's enough left over so that you can pay yourself.

Rule 5: Eliminate the word "free." By offering newbies a small discount as an incentive, you show them the value of what you do right away. Giving your services away for free de-values them; your clients may appreciate what they're getting less than if they'd paid a fee.

Rule 6: Set up a firm but client-friendly cancellation program. We use a 24-hour cancellation policy, however if a client lets us know even an hour or so before the class that they can't make it, we will always try to fill their spot with someone on the waitlist or another client. If we can fill the spot, we don't charge it against the client's account. If we can't fill it and the client sends someone in their place, that is great, too.

After speaking with me and exchanging a few emails after the conference, the studio owner with the $69 unlimited package changed her pricing structure and membership structure. She's now making money and not giving her services away!

## ~ Extra Membership Perks ~

For our super-committed and dedicated members, we add some extra perks while being careful that they don't hurt the profitability of the business. Below are some ideas. You don't have to do them all! Just pick a few that complement your business.

- 20% discount at the studio boutique or on any athleisure wear (if your studio offers it)
- 10% off the first package of Private/Semi Private Sessions
- 50% off a special program and/or workshop you offer
- $10 discount on second same-day class
- 1 guest pass per month for a new friend

We also give new members a small gift, like a branded canvas tote (no need to worry about sizing, as you would with a t-shirt), when they commit and join for a year. We fold the tote up, put the welcome card on top and tie it with ribbon.

## ~ Smaller Memberships ~

People often ask us for a deal or coupon or cheaper classes, so I offer a small monthly membership: a package of five classes for $99 that expires in 30 days. There are no ifs, ands or booties about this policy! This way people can commit to classes at a more affordable price and get all the perks of our Core Membership. Sometimes this program helps new clients become regulars because they know they only have 30 days to use up their classes.

Often, these clients end up spending even more, because they use the five classes up in a week and then buy another package because they've enjoyed their classes and can't go a whole month without exercise. An affordable entry-level package can convert a new client into a fully committed regular.

## ~ *Why should clients become members?* ~

Below are some benefits that you can highlight in your marketing to help your clients see the value of becoming a member of your studio:

- Added Perks. Members receive the discounts mentioned earlier and get free guest passes.

- Commitment. The membership will cost more than just a few classes so clients are likely to be incentivized to show up. And the more they do the faster they'll see results.

- Quality. Classes are smaller and the trainer in your studio is actually teaching (not working out at the front of the room), making sure you're doing the exercises correctly. This ensures that you'll get the most from your workout.

## ~ *Pricing and Packages that Work for Everyone* ~

Let's talk about these free intro sessions and other classes we create to get people to come through our doors.

In my opinion, the intro sessions should cost two or three times more than a regular workout. We have to work so hard during that first session to sell what we believe in and share our knowledge and expertise. We have to show our new client how we're going to help them reach their fitness goals. We spend extra time with them and may even give them handwritten exercises for homework.

One of the things that drives me nuts is when I see that people are offering first time clients FREE sessions or classes! When you get your nails done at a new nail salon do they give you a manicure for free? When you try out a new hair stylist does she give you a break? When you try a new restaurant do they give you a free meal? No! Then why are we offering FREE and discounted classes? If anything we should be charging more for that first session. We work so hard on making it perfect.

It is okay to offer a small discount to entice people through the door, but remember this is your job and you should get paid for being so awesome! Right from the start, train your clients to see the value of what you do. There is plenty of time later on for you to give back and thank your regulars.

April Walker (Lifetree Pilates) says, "Never undervalue your service and your business. People will always try to get you to lower your prices and discount your work. Stay strong and know your worth. It takes a lot of time, money and blood, sweat and tears to get certified, to open your own business and to stick to it. Don't forget you need to get paid for all of that. You're worth it. Have confidence in the work you've done and trust your gut. Sounds like a stupid cliché but it is sooooo true."

## CHAPTER 5
# Making Clients Comfortable with Fees

├────────────── • ──────────────┤

*"You can't just ask the customer what they want and then try to give that to them. By the time you get it built, they'll want something new."*
— Steve Jobs

"**D**id I charge too much?" "What if they don't think I am the real deal?" "Am I not good enough to ask for these prices?" Just stop! We all have bills and we all want/have to make our "bottom line" plus some extra in order to keep our doors open.

Money is a funny thing. Even people who have boatloads of dough have priorities when it comes to spending it. As studio owners, it's our job to show clients the value of what we offer, and explain why it's so important for them to invest in their health. Some will get it right away while others might take a bit more work before committing.

So how can we best accommodate our customers' budgets?

I had a new client who'd just moved to the area from Missouri, and she had finished her intro offer. She wanted to purchase a new package that day. Ms. Missouri asked what kinds of deals and coupons we were offering that week. She told me how much she loved

Pilates and said it was the only type of workout that made her feel strong, healthy and happy. She also mentioned that it was hard for her to afford classes once or twice a week. She knew how much the equipment and springs cost, how much time and money a certified teacher spends on their education, and the value of Pilates. She hated the gym, loved the small classes and individual attention, and needed a certified teacher due to a few spine and neck issues from a car accident. The only thing she didn't like about our classes was the price.

I handed her a menu of our package options and explained that the bigger the class package she bought, the less she'd be paying per class. Unfortunately, she didn't like any of the packages and, looking on her phone, asked if we were on any coupon sites.

I snapped: "If, God forbid, you ever need a hip replacement or emergency surgery, are you going to ask for the cheapest surgeon at the hospital?"

WHOOPS!! (Insert duct tape over mouth, staple lips shut!)

She actually stayed for class and afterwards I ran up to her and apologized for my outburst and tried to smooth things over. She apologized, too, and said she understood the quality and attention she was receiving in the classes and said she would continue to invest in her health. She is currently a regular and comes two to three times a week.

Not all scenarios end like this (especially with a crabby owner). We can get so protective of our businesses and snap because we take things personally. The incident with Ms. Missouri made me realize I needed a day off. Not everyone sees the value of what we do right away, so it's up to us to train them (in more ways than one) and highlight all the benefits they're receiving at our studios. You can also encourage clients by getting creative with pricing and fee structures.

How can we, as studio owners and teachers, go outside the box and offer more options that will allow the Ms. Missouris of our world to come regularly without feeling financial stress—while at the same time ensuring the studio doesn't lose money on the deal? It's in everyone's best interest to keep boutique fitness affordable, so below are some flexible options to make it easier for clients on a budget to commit to regular classes every week.

## ~ Bring a Friend ~

If anyone brings a friend to class they get a credit added to their account. The friend doesn't get a class for free, but is offered our group intro pack of 3 classes as well as the credit offer for any friend *they* bring in. This offer has brought in new people who have become recurring clients and then bring in their friends—it's a great way to encourage word of mouth without you having to be part of the conversation. Once a client brings in three friends, they've basically gotten a free class and you've gained three new clients and made revenue from their intro packs.

Our clients can get creative too: one of our regulars used all her $10 referral coupons to purchase private classes for a friend as a gift. Ideally, the ripple effect continues: that friend became another regular client of ours, and suggests us to her friends, and so on.

## ~ Create a Class ~

We offer clients the option to get a group together, decide what type of class they want, and pick a day and time (that doesn't conflict with the existing class schedule). We require at least four to six people for these classes and offer the group class package price, which they pay up front.

This way the studio and teacher are covered! These classes are great for groups of friends who are trying to get into shape together, for pregnant women and new moms looking to get back into shape, for bridal parties wanting to walk down the aisle as fit as possible, for birthdays or special occasions, and for beginners who are looking for a way to ease back into exercise slowly and somewhat privately.

## ~ Check-In Private ~

Sometimes our group class regulars, or groupies as we call them, want to get some extra attention and take a private. We offer these students a Check-In private in exchange for three already purchased group classes. Here's an example of our Check-In promotion:

*Are you a "groupie"? Fantastic! We love group classes, too, but if you're not quite getting your Teaser or Roll-Up, you have a chance each month to have a Private Session! Not only will you get 100% attention from one of our trainers, but you'll also get a discounted price without having to buy a whole package. Think of it as training for your body as well as a way to make your group classes even more productive.*

## ~ Payment Plan ~

The bigger the package, the cheaper each class, as I've mentioned. But for some clients, coming up with the full price for a big package at one time is a lot. In these cases we let the clients pay in two (or sometimes three) installments, as long as they are consistent with their workouts. We also make sure they realize that their package expires within three months and that there is no rollover. It's a win-win: We get paid and they pay for their sessions in an affordable and manageable way.

## ~ Check/Cash ~

Some credit card companies charge businesses up to 5% for processing fees. Add that to teachers' pay, wear and tear on equipment, electric bills and everything else, and we may not be left with a lot. Even though I believe that businesses should take credit cards, consider offering clients a small discount if they write a check or pay cash for their classes.

You can choose which credit cards to take. Everyone loves their points and miles, but some of the fees associated with these cards are insane for small business owners! Consider taking just two or three different cards.

### ~ Pilates Tab ~

We have private clients who like to take classes two, three or even four times a week, but coming up with funds for a large pack can be a challenge. We offer our hard-core regulars the same rate as a large pack, but let them pay whatever they can afford up front. They choose the amount and when their tab is gone, they replenish it as they go—we get payment up front before the sessions. Everything is kept track of in an old-school kind of way (pen and paper) on session cards that are kept in a box at the front desk. We also let them use their tab credit to purchase retail items (workout clothes, mats, etc.), water and snacks, if they have a positive balance and don't owe us money. As long as we are all getting paid on time, I don't care how we get paid. These clients are our regulars and we value them. They keep our doors open.

### ~ Shared Packages ~

Clients' marriages and certain friendships may be awesome outside the studio, but inside it's often best that partners, who may have different trainer preferences and need different exercise programs, exercise apart. We allow couples, siblings or good friends to share their packages even if they don't share classes. That way, they're shelling out money for 20 sessions (and they split it) rather than double the money for 40 sessions that they may not be able to use before the expiration period.

Now that you're equipped to help your clients afford classes without losing money in the process, keep in mind that there's a huge difference between "cannot afford" and "won't pay for!"

If clients try to bargain for a less expensive rate, stand firm. It's a slippery slope. As I've said before: you're providing an invaluable service as a teacher, coach and/or studio owner, and one that's worth every penny you ask for. (Assuming you haven't gone crazy with fees.) When in doubt, consider:

- Do you ask to pay less for a bottle of milk at the market? Or expect the clerk at the computer store to shave a few hundred bucks off the price of a laptop if you ask? When people tell me that Pilates—or babysitters, plumbers and hairstylists—shouldn't cost so much, I wonder if they'd feel the same if they were the ones doing the work. If you've fairly priced your classes, taking into account your overhead, there's no reason anyone should guilt you into lowering the cost.

- Besides: We're worth it. Our training wasn't completed in one weekend or online. Most of us have spent thousands of dollars and hours to get where we are. We travel for certifications, additional certifications, mentorships, workshops, continuing education, anatomy courses, etc. (My training education price tag exceeded my undergrad degree years ago.) All of that work is funneled into our studios and our teaching, and our clients are the beneficiaries. It's common sense that they pay for the exchange.

- The equipment we train our clients on is expensive! To fully equip a studio with the proper Pilates tools and equipment you're possibly heading upwards of six figures. Gyms and yoga studios also need equipment. In addition, we pay rent or mortgages, teacher payrolls, air conditioning and heating bills, maintenance on equipment and more.

- Pilates and boutique fitness classes are reasonably small to ensure our clients get the most from us and avoid injury. If your exercise regimen is one that can only accommodate a small number of students at a time (as is the case with Pilates), the only way you'll be able to make ends meet is to charge enough per person to stay afloat. If we had 30 reformers per class, it would make sense that those classes be less expensive.

At the end of the day we want to keep our classes full. We can always try incentivizing clients/students with packages that keep their budgets in mind, but don't undermine your value/worth in the process.

# CHAPTER 6

# Customer Service

|————————————————— • —————————————————|

*"Do what you do so well
that they will want to see it again."*
— Walt Disney

Customer service is a tricky topic. Even though the customer may not always be right, we have to remember that they are the customer. And they are paying us. (Translation: We need them.) So even though there are times we may want to scream in their direction, we have to learn to handle the situation as best as we can. How do we correct the customer without losing them?

Rachael Lieck Bryce prides herself on her customer service. "It's our number one way to retain clients, right up there with performance," she says. "I ask my staff to constantly reflect our sincerest appreciation with excellent customer service."

I'm guessing all of you with studios have at least one challenging client who, no matter what you do, remains unsatisfied. I have one who's been coming to the studio for years. She makes a habit of signing up for one class (sometimes taking a spot from someone on the waitlist) and then coming to a different one—and gets upset when she's charged for both, even though she *knows* that's our policy. (In part because we have to remind her of it week after week.) Add to that, she shows up late, always forgets her socks, and doesn't want to wear the ones we offer. She constantly cancels at the last minute and doesn't think she should be charged, even if we can't fill her spot. To top it off, she repeatedly asks for discounts (we repeatedly say no—in the nicest way) and "forgets" to pay for her water. Sound familiar?

How do I handle her? With a lot of deep breaths and good will summoned from deep in my core. Here are some tips to stay sane and sober in the face of excruciating and aggravating clients:

Know when to be flexible. One sunny Saturday we had a man walk into the studio after finishing his intro Power Pack of five private sessions and five group classes. It was time for him to buy a new package, and he wanted to get the same one—and continue to pay the intro price. Although we don't normally offer this particular combination of private and group classes outside the intro offer, I told him I'd make an exception, but the price would be a bit more. He appreciated the gesture—and thought he was a genius for instigating it. He signed right up. We put the new package on our menu of options and it became a favorite with other clients as well.

Shut mouth and open ears. My instinct is often to use my words before listening. But trying to understand why a customer is upset is crucial—their feedback is important, even if their complaints seem a little over the top. Sometimes all they really want is to be heard, and once that's accomplished, they'll settle down. Other times, they may have a valid point, which can change the way you do things—in a positive way.

Take it outside. I don't like confrontation in my studio, so if it looks like the client and I are going to be in a long discussion, I'll try to find a quiet spot, either a nook in the studio or, weather permitting, outside. The change of scene often helps take the charge out of the atmosphere, and also protects the rest of the clients from having to be part of the scenario.

Sometimes you have to slip into customer service mode when you least expect it. While waiting for a restaurant table one night (yes, it happens, occasionally I put on real clothes, even makeup, and have a life outside the studio…), I ran into a client who had stopped coming to classes for a while. I'd sent a postcard and an email and even left a message on her cell phone because she had group classes that were going to expire. But I hadn't heard back.

She was happy to see me and claimed she loved the studio but felt that some of the classes were too chatty, or too hard. The class times weren't working for her schedule and she was disappointed that she'd spent so much money on her class package. As she spoke, I kept my mouth shut, listened and did a lot of nodding.

When she (finally) came up for air, I asked if she'd like to exchange her remaining group classes for a private session—and promised we'd work out and not talk. She could schedule it whenever she wanted. Her eyes widened, like a toddler seeing their first birthday cake. She was back at the studio the following week.

Allowing her to vent gave me the opportunity to come up with a solution that worked for both of us. There is always a solution, we just have to find or create it.

Occasionally there may be a hiccough when an employee has a different idea of customer service than you, the owner, does. For example, years ago when a client told her trainer, one of my very first employees, that she was moving across the country and wouldn't be able to use all the sessions in her package, the trainer assured her I'd be happy to refund her for the unused portion.

Wrong!

The client wasn't too happy when I explained, as it says on our Liability/Health History form in big bold print, that we don't give refunds on purchased packages.

But I offered her two options: She could transfer the unused privates to her sister, who was also our client, or she could use the dollar amount of the classes in our boutique.

After calming down a bit, the client said she appreciated my honesty and used her credit to pick up some snazzy spandex numbers and soaking salts in the boutique. The cost ran a little over what she'd been allotted, and I ate the difference in the interest of keeping her happy—which she was when she left. When she comes back East to visit her family, she always stops in for a session.

Basic manners never go out of style. Listen to your clients with respect and consider a solution that will make them feel heard and appreciated.

You don't have to wait for a meltdown to show the love. Everyone wants to feel cared for and, as fitness professionals, that's an important part of what we do. To bolster the negotiation tactics described above, here are some evergreen courtesies that we make use of throughout the year. Maybe they'll spark some other ideas that will work in your studio.

- Give out mints, hair ties, fruit and other treats. Having some of these around the studio will add that extra positive perk for clients.

- Check-in on clients regularly, either in-person or with an occasional email. Ask how they're feeling, if they like their new class, if they have questions, etc.

- Show genuine interest in what your clients are doing or telling you.

- Ask for and accept feedback. It assures clients that your focus is on them, and it shows you where you can do better. There is always room for improvement.

- Respond quickly and directly to clients' questions, comments, complaints and requests. There are likely other studios nearby who'd love to accommodate them if you're slow on the uptake.

- Build a community. Introduce clients to each other, paying special attention to the newer ones (who may soon become regulars), and establish a friendly, non-competitive atmosphere before and after class.

- On the other side of building a community, be understanding if people just want to work out and not get involved with the social aspect.

- Keep it fresh. Regularly offer new events, workshops and programs. Boredom is a business killer and you want to create a space where boredom doesn't exist!

- Support your instructors. Morale has a trickle down effect, and you want it effervescent from top to bottom. Publicly compliment and help other trainers out. They'll pick up the idea and do the same. This fosters a comfortable, friendly environment that clients enjoy being a part of.

- Love your job. Even on difficult days you can keep your mindset positive with a little effort. The boss's mood has a way of setting the stage for everyone else, so put on your happy face (you can take it off when you get home, like a pair of too-high heels).

Even after all your bending over backwards, there will be some clients who just can't be mollified. In that case, it's time for The Break-Up.

Once upon a time, we had a woman at the studio who was miserable. Every time she came in she had a suggestion on how to make the studio, the teachers, the equipment, the classes, the décor, the retail and even the sock selection better. She started to annoy some of our (nicer) regulars so much that they were calling and texting me to see if this woman was signed up for certain classes. After the last class in her package, I pulled her aside and asked her to leave and not come back, which is never an easy conversation to be had. Of course she had already decided that she wouldn't be back because there were just so many things wrong with my studio.

As a studio owner, it's important to remember not to get frustrated with people like this. Difficult clients take up a disproportionate amount of your time and usually things work themselves out—or not. I once agreed to continue working with a woman who was troublesome—talked down to me, showed up late, and dismissed my instruction. Even though I'd seen the warning signs, it seemed easier to go on than confront her. Then one night I found myself crying as I sat down to dinner. Over an unpleasant hour with an unpleasant woman—not worth it!

How many exes do you have? How many horrible dates have you been on? I've been on a lot! You're not going to mix well with everyone. You are you. Anyone that doesn't find you agreeable isn't the best choice of a client. There have been times after initial sessions with a client that we both knew we weren't a good fit and parted ways. Sometimes these clients continue to come to the studio and just train with someone else, other times, they moved on. There will always be more clients. Nothing good comes of muscling through a relationship with one whose demands are overreaching. Avoid the headache and refer them to someone else!

# CHAPTER 7
# Train Your Clients

———————————— • ————————————

*"You are serving a customer, not a life sentence. Learn how to enjoy your work."*

— Laurie McIntosh, co-author of *A Mixed Bunch: 21 Cases For Diversity Training*

From the moment they walk through your door, you are training your clients. What rules do you want to instill (without sounding like your third grade teacher)? How do you make your policies sound nice and fluffy like a bunny without offending anyone?

What do we do when:

## ~ Clients Late Cancel ~

"My car won't start!" "My baby is throwing up." "I woke up with a nasty cough." "My dog has a hangnail."

We have heard it all! The last-minute cancel comes with a smorgasbord of excuses.

We get it, life happens. But when our clients can't make it to the studio we have a few solutions for those who cancel within 24-hours of class.

- We keep track on our online system and give a one-time get-out-of-jail-free card. (By August, clients are likely to forget they already used their free pass back in January.) If they question us, we can tell them the exact class, date, time and teacher.

- If clients have a membership program and prepay, we make sure they have a credit card on file. If they're no-shows or late cancel, their card will be charged the price of the class. If there is no card on file or the card has expired, the fee will be billed to their account and must be paid before the client takes another class.

- Clients have the option to send a friend or family member in their place. Who knows—maybe the happy recipient will love the class and come again.

- If we can fill the spot with someone on the waitlist or a walk-in, we won't charge the late-canceling client or count the class as taken.

## ~ The Client Wants to Extend an Expired Package ~

We give our clients three months to use their five and ten—class packs and six months to use their twenty—class packages. In my opinion, the expiration date keeps them accountable and coming to workout consistently. But sometimes studio owners get hit with clients asking to extend their class packages because they took the summer off or just got busy.

So how do we come up with a client-friendly policy that gives them options? We allow clients to extend their expiring package if they buy a new package. They have three or six months to use up the classes/sessions in both packages. If that's a no-go, they can gift the remaining classes to a friend.

### ~ *We Encounter Sock Resistance* ~

We require socks, which I'll get into, and sell them in our boutiques.

One day a client brought her friend to class and they both forgot socks. I kindly reminded them about our sock policy and offered socks for them to borrow. We always have a clean stash behind the desk. Instead, she grabbed two new pairs from the boutique, threw a bunch of cash down on the desk, and said, loud enough to be heard five miles away: "The reason Blondie requires us to wear socks here is so she has more money to do her hair every week!"

True story. Below are the real reasons why "Blondie" requires socks at her studios:

1. Hygiene. When I first opened Body Be Well I didn't require socks. But after my first time cleaning all the not-so-pleasant added debris off the machines and floors, I made socks a #1 priority (read: rule) Don't get me wrong, we clean the equipment after each use, however where your foot goes, your hand goes. There are germs everywhere and by wearing socks we can protect ourselves just that little bit more and keep everything tidier and cleaner.

2. Safety. We don't care if people wear socks with grips on the bottom, but it does help them from slipping around on the equipment. For those that don't have grip socks we offer grip mats, which provide the same extra assistance when working out.

3. Cold Feet. Living on the East Coast we can get snow and negative temperatures and even with heat on, the floors are still cool sometimes. During the summer, we have air conditioning.

4. Most studios have a strict no-shoe policy for the studio floor. If the thought of walking barefoot in a common area isn't your thing, socks are the ticket.

### ~ *Our Substitute Teachers Get a Grouchy Reception* ~

Everyone has to take time off at some point. Even I do! One weekend while I was away at my brother's college graduation (kind of a big deal) I got this email from a teacher:

> *Hi Chelsea,*
>
> *I hope you're having a fun time away. I just wanted to fill you in on what happened today. I had one woman leave class before we even started because she said I wasn't you, and then another woman acted so rude that I am pretty sure she hates my guts. She rolled her eyes so many times I thought she might be having a stroke in class. See you on Monday.*

As I mentioned earlier, it's important to train your clients to be gracious and open to substitute teachers. If you let them know that everyone helps each other out, it really goes a long way. Inevitably, emergencies or vacations come up, so substitutes are called in. It's our job to train our clients to be open-minded and welcoming when we can't be there.

When clients make it obvious that a substitute has made this their no good, terrible, horrible, very bad day, it's hard to rise above their rock bottom expectations. So it's important to prepare them in advance to appreciate what a sub can offer.

A few times a year I send out an email to all the clients reminding them about the upsides of a substitute—and asking them to behave.

Dear Clients,

If you've made it to class and decide to give the sub a try, be open to a new experience and smile. Yes we know this can be scary, but with a new teacher you might actually learn something new! You might finally understand what your favorite teacher was trying to say about "opening up your collar bone," or you might get that upper back release you've been looking for. We can easily get used to a certain teacher's style, let our minds and bodies become stale and fall into patterned movement. Get excited to have the opportunity to try something new. Even if the class isn't your favorite, you'll have learned something about what you do and don't like.

We all just want to help you! Exercise and fitness are supposed to be fun! So, if for some reason you're not loving the substitute, please try to hold back those eye rolls and heavy sighs and focus less on whatever is confusing or angering you and more on the teacher's intention, which usually is positive and compassionate—you know how picky I am about my instructors! We know you pay a lot at the studio door, but please be nice.

We want to make sure you are getting the most out of your workout with us and with substitutes. If something doesn't make sense to you or seems strange, ask us. We all want to make sure you understand our teaching style and us. See the teacher after class and ask why something was taught differently than the way you know. Given the many teaching styles and certification programs, people learn and explain things differently. Even if you stand by your original understanding, experiencing a new approach can be extraordinarily helpful.

Love,

Your "Favorite" Teacher

## ~ *We See Too Much* ~

Maybe some of you have had a client who dressed a little scantily. And by this I mean didn't bother with his or her undergarments, so you saw a lot more than their abs when they were training. No thank you! A girl once came to our studio braless in a white and tight t-shirt asking to do jump squats with one of our male trainers. I quickly showed her the bras in our retail section and suggested that she might want to purchase one before her session. We had a guy come in super-short shorts who wanted to stick to leg circles and a lying down workout (he was tired from his job, he said). So instead we did his whole workout standing and next time he showed up with long pants.

It didn't take long to realize we had to address the abbreviated wardrobe issue. We put signs in the dressing rooms:

Dear Fabulous Clients,

Please remember that during fitness we move, sweat and contort our bodies in all kinds of not-so-everyday positions. So please remember to keep everything covered and contained so we can do our job without any surprises!

Thank you,

Your Trainers

### ~ *Noses and Equipment are Assaulted: Perfume, Lotion & Zippers* ~

As Carrie Pages, an extraordinary Pilates teacher and studio owner in Wilmington, North Carolina says, "One of the biggest issues I've had is with perfume and essential oil use. While it always smells great to the person wearing it, we have some students with severe allergies. My first approach was an email to everyone with updates for the month that also included the concern about scented toiletries. We still had some who didn't make changes to their habits, so I made direct phone calls, which is never easy! I also took all scented sprays out of the bathroom."

Encourage your students to come fragrance-free to the studio and save the scents for other times.

Depending on your equipment, you may also want to encourage clients to come zipper- and snap free—in other words, to wear workout gear that won't rip or destroy your expensive machines and props. In the case of Pilates, you want to protect the leather of the reformers, and don't want clients getting hurt if their jewelry gets caught in the springs.

### ~ *Clients Balk at New Pricing* ~

Hopefully you've internalized my earlier rant about owning how much you're worth and not feeling chicken-hearted when it comes to charging fair prices. You can apply the same philosophy to raising class fees. There's no need to apologize for it, and if you're tempted, consider how much you're paying in rent (or mortgage), for electricity, water, cleaning, payroll, heat, air conditioning—all the seemingly beside-the-point costs that clients may take for granted.

Not much in this world costs less from one year to the next. (Okay, maybe potato chips…but not services!) When the time comes to raise your prices, just put up a sign in the studio—put it in a cute frame if you like—and be done with it. No biggie. (On the flip side, as I've mentioned, don't undercut yourself by dropping prices to compete with another studio down the block.)

The committed clients will understand, others may take a break but are likely to come back soon enough. If they don't, there are plenty of other fish in the sea. The ones who throw a fit and complain and then take a short sabbatical often come back. And if not they aren't meant to be at your studio anyway.

## CHAPTER 8
# Games & Parties Are Good Business

|———————————————— • ————————————————|

*"Think left and think right and think low and think high.*
*Oh, the thinks you can think up if only you try."*
— Dr. Seuss

The C-word, Community (not the "C" word you were thinking of?), is a key part of the studio business. But it's often overlooked.

Our clients, teachers and team are all united in our love of movement—the way it makes us feel, the strength it gives us, and maybe even the sweat it requires!

Yet, we can see that our studios are so much more than just places to work out. When I observe my team and clients together at Body Be Well, I am so happy to see and recognize this community we have all created.

I love watching people who didn't know each other just a few months before making plans to go on a walk, sharing recipes, or showing off pictures of their children, grandchildren and fur babies. After each class or session, I see a blossoming community, which allows me to take a deep breath and smile! How about you?

I began teaching Pilates to help people change and improve the way their bodies' function, something that makes my work deeply rewarding. The creation of community adds an even deeper level of fulfillment.

As you head into this chapter, think not only about the community you have created but also about what more you can do, above and beyond helping your clients take care of their bodies, to create fun and exciting programs to encourage your community continue to thrive.

Here are some fun programs we've offered to keep clients engaged and excited.

## ~ *The Challenge!* ~

Another C-word, and not always our favorite, right? It's pretty obvious to me, and I'm guessing, to you, that exercise should be a part of everyone's life. So I roll my eyes when I see "New Year's Weight Loss Challenge" or "Summer Skinny Boot Camp" promotions. Is the new year the only time we want to be healthy? Is summer the only time we want to be active and in shape? It seems to me that these seasonal programs or challenges encourage people to make drastic changes that rarely lead to healthy habits they can hold onto forever.

Challenges are great because they give students the opportunity to take part in a repetitive practice. How can you create challenges that don't just create more laundry?

Set Goals. Ask your clients to set goals aimed at making significant physical, nutritional and/or lifestyle changes. Encourage them to be realistic: hike a mountain, complete 50 miles on their bicycle in a certain amount of time, run a 5k race. By making the goals achievable, the clients will be invigorated by their success (and grateful to you for pushing them to a new level).

**Add a Time Frame.** A challenge with a specific start and stop date gives clients the motivation to add the necessary workouts to fulfill their goal. Most run about a month because of the often-cited 21-day rule; it takes 21 days to form a new habit. What they learn from the exercise might even be more valuable than a number on a scale or a clothing size label.

**Write it down.** During our challenges, we ask clients to write their goals down, and we post what they've written on a bulletin board so everyone can be reminded and inspired. Some write their names on their goals, others choose to remain anonymous, but each time they come into the studio the goal is there staring at them.

**Join In.** I'm a Pilates instructor, but I'm also human, and sometimes I don't want to exercise any more than anyone else. To ensure that I set an example for my clients, family and friends, I participate in my studio's challenges. I also give my team an extra perk or two to join in and up the challenge for them. They get a discounted rate and I also will make their prizes more personal. For example, one of my trainers loves a certain Mexican restaurant and another loves to get her nails done at a certain spa, so if they win I will get a gift certificate to one of their favorite places. In addition, whoever signs the most people up for the challenge gets a $100 credit towards their next workshop, at my studio or elsewhere.

So while I'm skeptical about one-off seasonal challenges, I'm all for getting involved with programs throughout the year that will push your clients and your team to go outside their comfort zones. Bringing some healthy competition into your studio will also help to build community. One year we offered a gift certificate to a local restaurant as one of the challenge prizes and two of the clients who won went together.

I challenge you to try a challenge!

## ~ *Making the Challenges Profitable* ~

Challenges are good for the body and the psyche. They can also be good for the bottom line. There are all sorts of creative ways to package and present challenges that encourage clients to partici-pate—and pay for the fun.

31-Day Challenge

The goal of the 31-Day Challenge is to see how many classes a client can take in 31 days. To encourage more privates, we also offer a slight Challenge discount on purchasing one private at a time. Those who can't get to group classes or are on the waitlist often opt for privates on those days.

To amp up the excitement, my sister, Shannon, who manages the studios and is also a teacher, makes a colorful Challenge Board out of foam poster board. Clients add stickers (I have stickers with our logo on them) alongside their names after each class or ses-sion they take. Everyone in the studio (and community) can follow along and see who is winning.

The best part is that after seeing the results of their extra work-outs, many clients don't want to stop the routine, so they continue with their packages—and in some cases buy larger ones and new memberships.

Along with the extra income that comes directly from the Chal-lenge, the studio benefits in future sales.

On the next page is a sample email you can send to your clients to get them excited about your 31-Day Challenge:

┝──────────────── • ────────────────┥

## ~ *B-I-N-G-O* ~

And Bingo was his name-o. You probably remember the song and the game, right? We have added "Be Well Bingo" to our studio and it's become a super-fun program that keeps our clients engaged, entertained and competitive.

To: ———

From: ———

Subject: ———

Dear Clients —

Welcome to our 31 DAYS OF (your exercise/yoga discipline here)! Congratulations on registering and taking the first step in reaching your fitness goals. We're all at (business name) because we have one thing in common...we love (type of exercise here). We love the camaraderie, the strength and (maybe) even the sweat! Here's an opportunity to up your game — and your fitness level!

31 DAYS OF (your exercise/yoga discipline here) isn't just a challenge. It's 31 days during which we encourage everyone to recommit to their goals, wellness, and living a healthy lifestyle. Let's try to eat clean, sweat more and stress less. I want all of you to get even stronger and stretch your body beyond the limits you thought you had. I want you to laugh more, breathe more, and have more fun! The goal of this challenge is so much more than just 31 days of classes. Think about what you want to accomplish this month. You might want to take one more class a week; you might want to take one class every day. Take it one step at a time and really go for whatever your goals might be!

I look forward to sweating and having fun with all of you.

You can order customized Bingo cards at buzzbuzzBingo.com that make sense for your business. When you place your order, you'll get the option to "scatter the board," meaning everyone's boards will be different. At the bottom of the game card, we list our rules and lay out the different ways to win.

Along with the boards, I purchased Bingo daubers to be extra fancy. We brought in a bunch of extra income in a month. As you can see from the photo, the card encourages clients to take privates, bring in their friends and purchase retail. The bottom line is that people can come as few as five times during Bingo month and still win a prize. This may also be a good time to offer or introduce a shorter/smaller membership for first-time visiting friends.

| B | I | N | G | O |
|---|---|---|---|---|
| PERFORM 100 JOE JACKS | CHECK-IN ON FACEBOOK OR INSTAGRAM | TAKE EVERY TEACHER'S CLASS | TELL US 5 PILATES EXERCISES NAMED AFTER ANIMALS | TAKE A CHECK-IN PRIVATE OR GET A MASSAGE |
| REVIEW US ON OUR FACEBOOK PAGE | NAME THAT TUNE WHEN YOUR TEACHER ASKS YOU | DEMO THE LONG STRETCH SERIES (all 4 exercises) | SHARE ONE OF OUR SOCIAL MEDIA POSTS | POST A PIC ON SOCIAL MEDIA AND TAG US IN IT |
| TAKE A FIELD TRIP TO YOUR NOT REGULAR BBW STUDIO | TAKE A JUMP BOARD CLASS | Body be Well Pilates | PICK AN ADVANCED EXERCISE & PERFORM 10 WITHOUT STOPPING | BRING A MAN TO CLASS |
| PURCHASE A PACKAGE | TAKE 20% OFF AN OUTFIT (top & bottom) | TAKE 5 CLASSES IN 1 WEEK | BRING A FRIEND TO CLASS | HOLD TEASER FOR 1 MINUTE |
| TAKE A CLASS ON SATURDAY & SUNDAY | WEAR ONE BBW SIGNATURE ITEM TO CLASS | PURCHASE A PAIR OF GRIP SOCKS | TAKE & PASS OUR PILATES POP QUIZ | BALANCE ON YOUR TOES FOR 30 SECONDS WITH YOUR EYES CLOSED |

Name _____
Complete a "bingo" 5-in-a-row either diagonal, up & down, or left to right and win an awesome prize! Complete an "X" on your board and win an even better prize and complete the whole bingo board and win an even more awesome prize! One card per person & limit one square marked off each day!

Prizes!

We couldn't forget about the prizes could we? I try to use as many local businesses as I can when coming up with prizes. My many neighborhood business friends and contacts have been happy to help me, even making special products to accommodate (my sometimes crazy) needs. It's a good opportunity for them to introduce or promote their products to my clients, and a great way for my clients to learn about their businesses.

Before heading online or to the big box stores for prizes, check out your own backyard. We give gift coupons to a local tea or coffee shop, for example, or a bottle of body lotion from a local maker. A cosmetic company we often work with created a small size pot of lotion just for us—so it would fit in our gift bags.

Don't be afraid to ask for a specialized size, flavor, or anything else. You're helping local businesses spread the word about their products, and giving them access to your fabulous clientele. We also worked with a local company to create branded piggy banks that say *Pilates Fund*. Another company made coffee mugs with our logo and "I like my coffee strong, just like my Pilates body" written on the side. A coffee shop made a special Body Be Well Blend just for us!

For people who work out every day of the challenge or fill out their entire Bingo card, we splurge on some larger prizes, such as cozy sweatshirts, gift cards to a local juice bar, and mini foam rollers that fit perfectly in a Bingo-themed wine bag. They cost a little bit more, but are well worth it as this is a great way to reward our most committed clients. (It is also an incentive for other clients to up their game next time.)

In addition to shopping local I also try to use products that help a greater cause.

For example, we include Good Spread Peanut Butter in many of our packages.

Good Spread was created by MANA Nutrition, a non-profit that makes a life-saving peanut butter medicine for children suffering from severe malnutrition. For every jar sold, Good Spread provides a packet of this therapeutic peanut butter to a malnourished child. How cool is that?

When packaging our prizes we use clear bags so the photos look intriguing on social media, and we tie them with colorful ribbons.

For special events, such as an open house, we might make scratch-offs to give to people as they walk in the door. They offer a variety of goodies, like a selection from our boutique, or a percentage off a class package or retail purchase.

We searched for companies that make custom scratch-offs, but they all required huge minimum orders and were expensive, so we made our own with gold, silver and glittery stickers we found online. They scratched off perfectly and were cheap. Score!

Other prizes we give:

- Manicure or pedicure from a local spa

- Grip socks

- Customized zip totes by online retailer Marcia Made It. All totes are affordable and can be customized to say whatever you want. Some of my favorites are "#GIRL-BOSS" and "You say Yoga, I Say Pilates" Marcia also makes one that says, "You say Pilates, I Say Yoga."

- Props (stretch bands, weights, etc.) that are used in classes

- Journals or notepads with motivational quotes

- Canvas reusable totes emblazoned with our logo (we also use these as gifts when clients become members or celebrate five years with us)

- Gift certificate to a local smoothie, juice, tea or coffee shop
- Branded (or not branded, but cool) water bottles

## ~ *The Workout With Take-Out* ~

In some classes, in fact, in a lot of classes, we get on the topic of food. These conversations got me thinking of a way to combine food and exercise to entice new people to come into the studio. After a morning of teaching and brainstorming with one of my good friends and teachers, Elsah Epstein, we came up with the *Workout and Take-Out* program. It has become a huge hit!

We partner with a local restaurant and work with them to get a discounted rate on a selection of meals, usually three to simplify the ordering process. Then we offer our clients an evening class that includes take-out from the restaurant. The clients choose their dinner a day beforehand and it's waiting for them when class ends. They can either take it home or hang out and enjoy their meal with us. Some clients bring friends who shop at the boutique and even wind up buying exercise packages.

We charge a flat rate for the *Workout and Take-Out*. If people just want the workout or the take-out, the cost is half-price for either. The teacher also gets a flat rate for the classes no matter how many people sign up, and in addition, I buy their dinner. The balance of the profits goes to the business. While we're at it, we try to make it a fun night for everyone, offering a flash sale in the boutique and sometimes Champagne. Because what's a night out without a new pair of leggings and some bubbles?

On the next page is a sample letter I've used to ask local restaurants to collaborate with me.

Hi (name of restaurant),

I'm very excited to reach out to you. As you probably know, I own the Body Be Well Pilates studios in Red Hook and Catskill and I'm always eager to collaborate with awesome local restaurants!

I pride myself on giving 110% and love working with people who do the same. I believe that you fit this description.

So where am I going with this? After brainstorming with one of my team members, we came up with the "Workout & Takeout" idea. The concept is to get people to eat delicious, healthy food and move with an effective and practical workout like Pilates. I'd like to partner with you and offer my clients and (hopefully a lot of new people) the opportunity to come and take a class, ask questions, and see what Pilates is all about. Then, if you're in, they will finish with your great food!

So what I would need from you is a menu of three different healthy dinner options that my clients could pick from. The menu doesn't have to be complicated and it is up to you whether you want your food hot or not. I take payment ahead of time and will get you the food orders within whatever period of time you need. You would then drop off the meals after class. I'd give you a price per head—we can discuss the finances—and cover marketing and promotion. Also, we could cross-promote the event on social media.

Looking forward to hearing your thoughts and I thank you ahead of time for considering this opportunity!

## ~ *Parties* ~

Remember when you were little and you got invited to birthday parties at the bowling alley, roller rink or maybe a dance or karate studio? Well why not offer your clients the opportunity to hold birthday parties, bachelorette/bachelor parties or other celebrations at your studio?

At Body Be Well, clients can get a group together and invite them to the studio to take a class. Depending on your space and equipment, you can limit the number of people permitted to attend. The organizer picks the type of class they'd like, and we set up a time and day that works for everyone (including us). Then we host a class for the group. If the client wants to bring cake or something else to celebrate with after the class, we'll leave time for that as well.

We've had people bring in their own treats and we've supplied a few bottles of Champagne (for after class). For an additional fee, we'll work with other local businesses to provide the food and drinks for post-Pilates celebrations.

One time, a group chose to order juice and some grain bowls from a local juice bar, so we preordered everything and had it delivered for after class. Since the night included food, juice and a workout, we charged 10% above the cost of the food and the usual price of a class.

We'll give the birthday girl, bride–to-be or host her class for free (yes, I said free — even I can make an exception). If the party brings their own food, we just charge the normal price of a class.

A themed party is great for weekend specialty classes or celebrations. We did one we called Mats, Mimosas and Muffins for the fifth anniversary of one of our studios and had a lot of fun. People paid for their regular class and we supplied homemade muffins (baked by my wonderful sister, Shannon), mimosas and mocktails (for abstainers).

## ~ *Giving Back* ~

As business owners and teachers, we have a responsibility to give back to the community. We can enlist our clients and communities to join in the effort.

A program that our clients have embraced is Share What You CAN. Clients bring in three non-perishable food items in exchange for a class—we provide bins. Our clients are so generous, and most bring in way more than the three cans or packages of food requested. They've brought bags of everything from pasta and shampoo to toothpaste and tuna. At the end of the month we take the food to a charity in need. Being able to donate the food to a battered women's shelter is worth every free class we give out.

Another option to consider if you aren't a big studio is holding a free class open to anyone who donated.

## ~ *Holiday and Seasonal Promos* ~

Themed games—the sillier the better—are great ways to keep the studio light and fun and to get clients chatting with each other. Here are some ideas that have been popular for us.

Grab a container and fill it with a type of candy that suits the time of year or an upcoming holiday. Put some paper and pens out with an empty bowl for people to put their guesses of how many pieces of candy are in the container. Let your clients and team guess their hearts out!

Around Valentine's Day, hide a few glittery hearts under random mats and equipment. At the end of class, ask clients to look under their equipment—if they find a heart, they get a prize.

Around Easter, stuff plastic eggs with mini protein bars, headbands, hair ties, scratch-off lottery tickets, or whatever's small that strikes your fancy. Each time a client comes to class, give them an egg. The more classes they take, the more goodies they get. We put together a certain number of eggs for each studio and when they're gone they're gone.

Since my drawing skills and patience level are not that great, I had my sister's husband, Andy, draw pumpkin faces with a marker on clementines for Halloween treats. I also bought mini hand-sanitizers and attached a tag to them that said, "Germs are scary." Our clients were quite amused.

## ~ *Raising Your Profile* ~

The Check-In Challenge is a great way to encourage clients to help your studio gain more visibility on social media. Every time they check-in, tag, or write a review about your studio, have them put a slip of paper with their name in a jar at the front desk. At the end of a week or a month—whatever time frame you choose, have a drawing and give the winner or winners a little gift. It's as easy as that!

Whether you're launching a new program, promoting a contest, or just giving things away, the goal is to keep your clients, the newbies and the lifers, engaged and excited and looking forward to returning to the studio.

## ~ *Referrals* ~

You probably have tons of happy clients wanting to spread the word about how awesome you are and refer you to their friends and family. So how can you create a program that encourages these referrals but is also affordable and practical for you as a studio owner?

There are many online loyalty software programs that use a point system to keep track of your clients' activity, however some of the monthly costs are expensive. If you decide to use one of these, you'll have to determine how your clients will earn points and how many points they'll need to earn something. These programs can be a challenge to use. They also have the potential to be time-consuming for a small business owner. Be careful in deciding on which software to adopt. You don't need another administrative headache.

An alternative to the software route is the tiered program—clients have to pass through different levels before they earn their reward. For example, maybe your client earns $25 after their first five approved referrals (those who actually come and take class and purchase their class or package). Then they would hit the next tier, where they would earn $50 for every referral after that.

If you don't have the finances for a similar tiered program, maybe loyalty points are a better idea. For example, you can create a points-based loyalty program in which five referrals are worth 50 points and the client gets a special customized gift. Ten referrals, or 100 points unlocks a one-on-one session or maybe a gift card to one of their favorite shops or restaurants (another way to involve local businesses).

Another option is to offer a commission for referrals, which can be redeemed at your studio. We have given clients a credit worth 15% of what their referred family and friends purchase within 180 days of the first referral coming through our doors. As soon as the client has accumulated $50 in store credit they can claim their gift card. It's up to them if they want to spend it or continue to accumulate more cards to spend on larger purchases.

Below is an email we send to our clients, a fun example of how to introduce them to your new referral program:

To: ———
From: ———
Subject: ———

We really like spending time with you! We've got a great thing going and we want to work with more great people like you. We figured the person most likely to know more people like you, is, well, you. Let your good friends in on a good thing and refer them to (Name of Your Business).

We're all in different situations and need to do what works for us. The bottom line is that you want to come up with marketing ideas that do double time by showing your clients how grateful you are.

# CHAPTER 9

# The Magic Of Thank You

⊢———————— • ————————⊣

*"As we express our gratitude, we must never forget
that the highest appreciation is not to utter words, but
to live by them."*
— John F. Kennedy

Gifting is tricky. How many times have you opened a present
and thought, "Really? What the heck were they thinking?
Is this a re—gift? Do they even know me?" Cheap, cheesy and
unoriginal are three things you don't want linked to your gifts.

There are many times throughout the year when we might want
to buy our clients a special and meaningful gift. It may be for a
holiday, a birthday, their tenth year anniversary at your studio, or
maybe just a thank you for their consistent business and referrals.
There are so many holidays throughout the year, and I'm not saying
to celebrate every one with gifts for your clients, but picking one or
two will make them feel appreciated!

Here are the pros and cons of gifting.

Pros:

- Shows clients how grateful you are for their business

- Sends a personal message that you really appreciate them as people and not just as part of your business
- Showcases your creativity in a fun and engaging way
- It's just a nice thing to do.

Cons:

- Potentially makes us look needy and unprofessional. Plumbers, doctors and roofers don't give their clients gifts.
- Creates an awkward situation if your clients didn't give you anything

Keeping the potential snags of gift—giving in mind, I like presents that are light-hearted and relatively inexpensive, so they're not overly analyzed and nobody's put in an uncomfortable position.

So how do we make our clients feel special all year round without breaking the bank or going broke? As every year wraps up and we begin to plan for the one ahead, I am faced with the following questions:

- What should I give clients?
- How much time and money should I spend?
- Should I give them anything at all?
- Should private/semi-private clients get something more expensive or meaningful than group class clients?
- Do I give a gift to everyone who walks through the door—even brand new clients?

Private and semi-private clients have a special place with you. You spend many hours with them and know not only about their bodies, but their families, hobbies, kids and anything else they volunteer to tell you during their sessions.

You probably know their favorite restaurants, where they get their nails done, if they have a favorite brand of coffee or tea, if they like or don't like wine, and whether they enjoy movies. I give these clients a gift of some sort.

At the end of the day, choosing a gift depends on the client and what you can and feel like giving. Here are some other things to consider:

- How easy (or difficult) are they?
- How much do you enjoy teaching/spending time with them?
- How long have you been working together?

Some of the individual gifts we've given include gift certificates for restaurants and mani—pedis, necklaces made by one of my favorite designers, totes made by my grandmother, CORE wine, and Pilates Nerd totes with a pair of leg warmers.

We also show our appreciation on a group level by having events that are open to everyone who comes to the studios. For example:

## ~ *The Thank You Party* ~

Holiday parties don't have to happen at the end of the year. There's so much going on around that time already, it can be nice to throw an April Fools party or something out of the ordinary to switch things up. If you throw a Thank You party during a less busy time of year, your clients may be more likely to come.

Yes, parties can be expensive, especially by the time you buy food, beverages, napkins, plates, and silverware, and maybe even goody bags or door prizes. Oh. Did we mention garbage and clean—up crew? Don't forget extra toilet paper and paper towels and soap. Think about whether your party will have a theme, which will require specialty decorations and scenery. And don't forget your outfit, hair and nails for the evening. Geeeeez!

Also, expect the unexpected—and sometimes downright rude. One time, a lady, not even a regular client, brought her own container and filled it to the top with all my delicious food before leaving with her free goody bag! Not kidding!

Still, at the end of the day, these events can be super awesome and FUN. They can also bring in new business and your regulars and dedicated clients will *sooooo* appreciate it. Not to mention the more bubbles you pour the more people will shop (if you offer retail).

Depending on the type of party and time of year, think about giving your soirée/festivities/shindig a name and make sure it's something that stands out and gets people curious and excited. Keep in mind that the event doesn't have to take up an entire afternoon or evening—it can just be an hour or two. You may also consider incorporating a special class and even a new collaboration with a local business.

Here are some names I've used for theme parties:

- Sips, Springs & Sweets
- Sip & Shop
- Pilates & Prosecco
- Cocktails & Contrology (from Alycea Ungaro's Real Pilates)
- Oh What Fun
- Fitness, Food & Fun
- April Fools—We aren't fooling!
- Brunch & Burn
- Muffins, Mats & Mimosas
- Smoothies & Springs
- Jump Board & Juice
- Cardio & Cocktails
- Spa & Springs
- Mimosas & Markdowns
- Sculpt & Sip

A Few Other Things to Consider…

Photographer. Maybe you know someone who's good with a camera, or you can hire a professional to get photos of everyone all dressed up (and not in spandex). After the party, you can make copies of the photos and frame them as gifts for your regulars for an upcoming holiday, birthday or special event. Our clients are very happy with their photo gifts.

Parties are a great opportunity to show current clients and perhaps new clients what you, with or without the equipment can do. Invite your team and trainers to not only come and have fun, but also to work out and demonstrate exercises.

Scratch Offs. Great door prizes! As soon as your clients and their guests come in, give them a custom-made scratch-off. These can give different percentage amounts off retail, bring a friend to class for ½ price, get a free pair of socks with $100 purchase, or anything else that fits your brand and business model. As I mentioned earlier, you can get scratch-off stickers in all different colors (even glitter) inexpensively. Get your promo scratch-offs printed, grab a marker and customize each one. A lot of printers have a minimum of 50 or 100, so by having the ability to do it yourself you can have many different options with these and then stick a scratch-off sticker right over your "special."

Goody Bags. The Goody (or Swag) Bag is a great enticement to get people through the door. Hang onto them until guests leave, so they have their hands free during the party. Partner up with some other local businesses that complement you and your studio. Maybe a client makes something delicious. Does a local spa make an amazing face scrub you can't live without? For one holiday party, Topical Bio Medics, a local business which makes the topical pain reliever Topricin®, offered us tubes of their Sports Cream which we bagged in small gift bags and sealed with custom-made "Thank You" stickers.

## ~ *Movie Night* ~

This idea came from studio owner and teacher, Carrie Pages of Carrie Pages Pilates in Wilmington, NC. "We had a movie night where we watched the Joe Pilates movie," she says. "It was fun to share all of the nerdy knowledge with our clients and help them realize they are part of something bigger than just an exercise program." Do you have a fun movie, or a motivational speaker or educator who will teach your clients more about what you (and they) do? This is a nice way to bring everyone together and, again, you can invite other businesses to participate, and have healthy (or not so healthy) snacks available—because everything is better with food!

## ~ *Gifting Local* ~

How many times do we stress the idea of shopping local? It's been said that if each of us spent $100 a year more on local businesses instead of chain stores, it would put an extra $3 million a year into our economy and create thousands more jobs every year. Living in the Hudson Valley, I'm so lucky to have lots of local businesses that are happy to work with me on customizing some pretty awesome stuff!

Look at which products you use and love and go from there. Or maybe a client sells a product. Is there a local charity or community event it makes sense to partner with, one that would bring awareness of the studio to the community and awareness of the event to the studio? Cross promotion is a great tool—everyone wins.

## ~*DIY and Delicious* ~

Sometimes you don't even have to go out of the house to create a gift! I came up with the Pilates Crack Snack after I'd bought a ton of equipment, expanded my space and spent scads of money on wallpaper. In a nutshell, I was broke! Been there before? After brainstorming with my sister and mom, we agreed to make one of my mom's famous snack mixes, throw it in plastic goody bags with custom tags, and tie them with a ribbon. Voila — our holiday present.

I was so worried that people weren't going to like it and that it wasn't healthy enough, but it's still one of our clients' favorite things! Below is the original recipe.

Pilates Crack Snack

Ingredients

1 box Golden Grahams Cereal™

1 box Cracklin' Oat Bran Cereal™

1 box Quaker Oatmeal Squares™

3 boxes of Teddy Grahams™ (3 different flavors)

4 cups sweetened banana chips

4 cups vanilla yogurt raisins

3 bags M&M'S® (plain, peanut, peanut butter)

3 cups cocktail peanuts

3 cups honey roasted sesame sticks from the local health food store

Assembly

1. In a large bowl mix all the ingredients.
2. Divide and put into individual bags, then seal or tie with a ribbon. Add a tag (optional).

## ~ Branded Zip Pouches ~

I designed some cloth pouches and had them made up and printed with our logo and the phrase "I will not forget to do my Pilates 100," over and over and over again. We put two tea bags (two different flavors) from Athletea and a small sample of lemon-peppermint Fabulous Foot Cream from one of our local businesses, Hudson Valley Skincare. Then we popped custom tags on the pouches and gave them out.

### ~ Custom Coffee + Mugs ~

We partnered with a local coffee shop, JB Peel, and they ground pounds of a unique blend of their house-roasted coffee for us at a discounted price. We bagged the blend in half-pound resealable bags and put on stickers saying *Body Be Well Blend* beneath JB Peel's label. We've also made some custom mugs and paired them with the coffee for some of our private clients.

### ~ Good Spirits ~

CORE! How many times do we say, see, hear and live this word day in and day out? Well what could be more appropriate (or inappropriate depending on what you believe in) than a mini bottle of CORE vodka or gin for a gift? We tie a peppermint stick around the bottle with some ribbon and hand them out to our clients around the holidays.

### ~ Home Grown Gifts ~

Lots of people (not me) have a green thumb.

What if you have a garden that grows an enormous number of tomatoes and zucchini? Maybe you have chickens laying so many eggs you don't know what to do with them all. (This may sound like a #countrygirl problem—not applicable to most of you in cities, but it happens!) Regift Mother Nature's bounty—clients love home-grown edibles. Not only are you not wasting or throwing away your goods, you're making a client feel happy and appreciated.

### ~ Off the Cuff Gestures ~

How many times have you been running around doing errands when you stop at a local cafe or juice bar and run into one of your clients? When I do this, I like to buy their coffee, drink or juice. It's something small that makes a big difference. The total cost isn't a lot, but will make clients feel appreciated.

One of our regulars has taken private classes every Monday and Friday at eleven a.m. for the past seven years. I know he sometimes goes to lunch at a local café down the street from the studio. If it comes up during our session that he is headed there, I've called down to the cafe ahead of time and paid for his lunch. Little things like this can make a big impression.

## ~ *Acknowledging the Big Days* ~

Birthdays, engagements, weddings and anniversaries come up every year. Try as best as you can to make everyone feel special.

We found a company that makes packs of gum in special flavors and packages them with names like Birthday Cake, Wedding Cake and Red Velvet. We keep these behind the desk and give them to clients on their birthday (if we know), anniversary or other special occasions.

## ~ *Hello, Baby!* ~

A child is born every 7.4 seconds in the U.S., so there will likely be times when you'll have the pleasure of knowing clients and team members who are expecting a child. This is, of course, a special time for them, whether it's their first or fourth child. We designed blue and pink onesies that say *My Mommy Does Pilates,* and stamped our logo on the backs.

We also make up onesies that say, *My Grammy Does Pilates*, *My Aunt Does Pilates*, *My Dad Does Pilates* and so on. They're easy to customize, so you can make it appropriate for each client.

We package the onesie together with a tea from Pink Stork, a company that specializes in teas that help pregnant ladies overcome morning sickness and improve their prenatal health. We also love a mommy-and-me nail polish duo from Ella and Mila that we give to clients we know are expecting a girl.

## ~ Handwritten Thank You Notes ~

Sometimes simple is best. When was the last time you received a handwritten thank you note from anyone? A handwritten note is so powerful for a small business in so many ways. Your client will know that you took the time to go that extra mile. This will not only strengthen your relationship with them, but also help you stand out from your competitors.

Sample #1

Dear Client —
Thank you for all your sweat, dedication and hard work this year! So grateful to have you at the studio!

Sample #2

Dear Client —
Thank you for shopping local and supporting your spandex addiction with us. We love the new pair you added to your collection this week and please feel free to let us know what you think of them. Thank you and enjoy!

## ~ *Email Blasts* ~

At certain times of year, sending an unexpected email reminding clients how much you appreciate them reinforces their relationship with you and the studio. If writing's not your thing, here are samples that you can tweak and make your own.

Sample #1

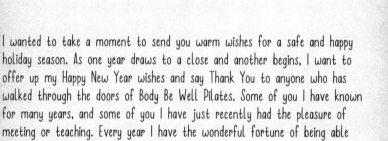

To: ~~~~~
From: ~~~~~
Subject: ~~~~~

I wanted to take a moment to send you warm wishes for a safe and happy holiday season. As one year draws to a close and another begins, I want to offer up my Happy New Year wishes and say Thank You to anyone who has walked through the doors of Body Be Well Pilates. Some of you I have known for many years, and some of you I have just recently had the pleasure of meeting or teaching. Every year I have the wonderful fortune of being able to work, learn, share and grow with you, and I am truly grateful to you for choosing Body Be Well Pilates as your partner in helping you gain strength and lead a healthy lifestyle.

So as we bring this year to a close, let's take a quick moment to think back over the past twelve months, to all the passion, determination and commitment towards a happy and healthy Pilates life you have created. I sincerely thank you. I am so lucky to call you clients and friends, and I wish you the happiest of holidays and a healthy and hard-core New Year!

Sample #2

To: ------
From: ------
Subject: ------

Here at Body Be Well Pilates I love the holidays because I get the chance to express my sincere gratitude to you, our amazing clients, and to our team of dedicated teachers. Many of you I have worked with for years, and some of you are new. I welcome each and every one of you. Each of you has played a big part in getting Body Be Well Pilates where it is today and where we will be going in the near future. We have lots of exciting things planned for the next few months and I can't wait to share them all with you!

So, thank you for your continued loyalty and commitment. Due to your many referrals we have been able to keep our studio full of fabulous people like you because they are your friends and family! And because of that we have been able to do a lot of great things this year. We

kept our group class rates the same

pulled all newspaper and magazine advertising to rely solely on your referral program (we give you $$$ for bringing family and friends to us)

added new equipment, got new carriages for all of our Reformers and new springs on all the Springboards, Reformers and Cadillacs

hosted even more workshops and trainings

upped the ante on our Pilates challenge prizes, offered more Pilates gifts throughout the year, and partnered with more local Hudson Valley businesses

My wish for you for this coming year is that you focus on all the positive that you do and have done. This goes hand-in-hand with your Pilates practice. Breathe and don't be so hard on yourselves. If you couldn't get Teaser this week don't worry about it. Progression, not perfection, is key!

I recognize you for everything you do for your family, your friends and your colleagues. Let's move, breathe, have fun and try to spring even higher than before!

# CHAPTER 10

# Making Retail Work

├─────────────────── • ───────────────────┤

*Life is short. Just buy the leggings.*

To spandex or not to spandex? Athleisure Wear. Yes it's a thing: versatile athletic clothing that looks good beyond the studio and can be worn out and about after class. We're all busy and sometimes just want to run from class to the bank to the grocery store and look presentable in the process—not like we just rolled off a treadmill. Selling athleisure wear at my studios has created a welcome source of income for the business and provided my clients with some great looking gear.

Before you take the leap, ask yourself these questions: Are your clients interested in studio retail? How much risk are you willing to take? How much extra work will this make for you? Do you have staff to support the shop?

There are 168 hours in a week. The average studio has a small percentage of time to generate income and another fraction of time to do everything else. Adding new classes, more clients or extra hours is not always the answer to generating more moula.

I want to help you decide if retail is for you. If it is, it will help you develop predictable additional revenue and added value for your clients.

Retail takes planning, support and constant investing. It requires careful decisions and staff who are willing to help and also learn about the products you choose to sell. When done well, retail can be an integral part of a successful studio's business plan.

At Body Be Well, the Pilates business is mine and the retail portion of the business is a separate company that I share with my sister, Shannon, splitting the work, cost and profit. When I started my company, I did it all alone and it was overwhelming. I just didn't have enough time for everything. By adding Shannon as a business partner, I divided the amount of tagging and hanging, paperwork, ordering, creative input and product—finding in half. The operation has been working and growing nicely. Remember that, like any business, it will require time and energy.

If you are unsure, it may be worth an experiment. Start small with one or two possible items placed near the front desk. Educate teachers and front desk staff on the products and see if they sell. Did they draw your clients' attention and wallets?

If you decide to go for it, there are many things that you can do to make your retail business successful. The upside of retail, including workout props or branded merchandise, goes well beyond income. It also nurtures deeper connections with your clients and offers them an easy way to shop local and support a business they love. Not to mention that it's convenient for them to have workout clothes and accessories available at the studio—especially if they come to class and realize they forgot their gear. It's super cool when you can sit back and watch your retail area enticing clients to get more involved with their practice and inter-act more at your studio. Retail can even foster camaraderie among clients as they provide each other with product recommendations and tell each other how good they look in their new leggings or tops. It's also fun (and funny) when clients come in wearing the same pair of leggings!

Karen Ellis, also know as Chief Pilates Nerd® says, "I don't have a big retail space in my studio, but I can tell you that when people finish a session and they feel wonderful, they like to celebrate or reward themselves with a fun item! I get excited for them, too."

Depending on where you're located, there might not be an athleisure store on every corner. In that case, people that are not clients may even stop in to shop. Maybe clients or someone local forgot about a birthday gift they need for their super yogi friend. Maybe the holidays are coming and they need some good gift ideas. Retail has the potential to reach beyond your regular clients and help boost your studio's revenue.

So now you've made the decision to sell retail. What the heck should you sell? Where do you begin? How do you know what will fly off the shelves? Sometimes what we think will sell doesn't, and sometimes what we sample or try out is gone before we know it. Anyone can carry product, but to find the right product can be tough.

My sister and I carry quality products that fit with our own lifestyle, clothing and accessories that we'd happily take home ourselves. In addition to working with local businesses, our emphasis has been on working with companies that give back, like beyondBeanie, a brand that donates a portion of the profits from each item (knitted hats and bracelets) to a child in need. We also look for unique pieces that clients can't find online or in the boutique down the road.

Before You Start Shopping

- Be creative about what you buy and make it relevant for your clients. Branded items such as t-shirts, sweatshirts and sweatpants are always a given for your retail line. Offering clothing and items that you believe in and wear yourself is also key. Why sell stuff you don't like?
- Know who's shopping. For example, most of our clientele do not wear crop tops and sports bras when they

work out. They like comfy attire that's versatile and can be worn all day long. Tank tops can also be a hard sell and some mesh can be awesome, but too much is not so good—a lot of people don't like to show off everything while working out. Some women like to cover their arms and backsides all year round, so we offer long-sleeve tops and shirts that are a little longer. If we are on the fence about a product, we'll ask a few clients for their opinion.

- Find brands and companies that will work with and for you. There are plenty of companies out there that want to sell you their merchandise. There is usually a basic wholesale form that you'll fill out with your tax ID number, the address of your business and some other basic information. Sometimes the application is a little lengthy and the company might even require photos and an interview. For us, that's too much work and time. Unless we're really over the moon about their products, jumping through too many hoops is a roadblock and we usually pass. We also pass when high minimum orders (often to the tune of thousands of dollars) are required. Be picky about whom you choose to work with. It's worth attempting to negotiate. A lot of companies will break their standard policy to accommodate smaller companies.

- What do you teach? What do your clients need for class or their sessions? Do you require that your clients wear socks? Sell them. Do you want your clients to wear zipper-free clothing so your equipment doesn't get damaged and clothing without strings or fringe so they don't get caught in a spring while working out? Sell items like that. Do you ask your clients to come fragrance-free to class? Don't sell stuff they can't use in your business.

- At Body Be Well we sell handmade zip pouches made by our Oma (grandmother in German and Frieda to everyone else). No one else has these to sell and each one is unique. People buy them to put gift certificates in, to carry their grip socks or just as a last minute gift. We sell a lot of these. By making your retail section unique you will keep your clients engaged and pleased.

- Offer a few different branded clothing items that clients can wear inside and outside the studio. Consider introducing something new at the beginning of a new season or around the holidays. For example, we offer new long-sleeve shirts with our logo on one arm in the fall when people are switching out of their t-shirts and into something a little warmer. Around the holidays we introduce some really great and comfy sweatpants with our logo on the left hip. Branded clothing is great because when clients run to the grocery store after class they are advertising for you and raising awareness in your community.

- Be sure to plan ahead. As Karen Ellis says, "The most frustrating thing about creating your own branded retail is that you can only produce it in a timely manner if the companies you work with do as well. This is an ongoing challenge, from graphic artists, to retailers of all products, to printers. I have lost my cool on more than one occasion!"

- Props and tools are a great sell because, as I mentioned before, when our clients work out outside the studio their time inside the studio will be even more effective. You're not just selling them workout tools, but also helping them incorporate exercise into their daily life. Foam rollers, toning balls and bands are just a few of the items that you might want to sell.

- Are there fitness and healthy lifestyle magazines or books you love? Share them with your clients. It's gratifying to watch them go home with new props and hear how they are using them, or hear that they tried a quick workout from a book they bought at your studio. You'll even hear that your clients are getting their family members moving too!

- Make your retail operation as easy on yourself as possible. Try to keep your selection organized and resist the temptation to offer lots of the same product in every single color. Just stick to the most popular pieces and be happy that when they're gone, they make room for new and appealing stuff. Also keep a few things that are your staples and make sure the companies that stock them have them available for instant purchase.

- Offer a wide range of prices. Our lowest priced item is a hair tie for $2.50 and our highest priced item is a pair of leggings for $98. If all your products are in the high price range, clients may be less likely to buy more than one thing because the dollars will add up quickly. Instead, cater to all budgets. You can have smaller, less expensive things like hair accessories, socks, candles, protein bars and other impulse buys near or on the front desk where clients pay, while also stocking pricier athleisure apparel for people who want to do more serious shopping. Variety is key.

- Consider promoting products on social media. We've sold to people across the U.S. through our posts and sometimes offer free shipping as an added perk.

- Featuring a Product of the Month has become really fun and also helps with sales. We place it right by the front desk where everyone can see it, along with a written description and a reason or two about why we picked it. Clients know there will be something new each month and look forward to it.

- Put little reminders around the studio to remind clients that when they look good, they feel good. Here's one we used:

  - *On the days when you're not in the mood to move, find your newest pair of leggings and put them on. By pulling on your spandex you're already halfway there. You can also make buying a new outfit a motivational reward to yourself— tally up how many classes you've taken in a week or month and reward yourself with a new top or pair of leggings when you reach your goal.*

- Staff discounts and membership perks will hopefully get your trainers to wear retail items from your boutique, which is a good way to subtly promote sales. Clients tend to admire their trainers, so seeing them modeling the clothing and gear you offer in the store is a simple and logical strategy to influence your clients to buy.

- Develop a simple system for re-ordering. Most companies will email you months ahead of time to pre-order the fall, holiday, spring, summer, etc. line. (We shop for our holiday order in May!) However it wouldn't hurt to mark it on your calendar, set up auto-replenishment, divide up duties between partners. Figure out what system works best for you.

## ~ *Boosting Sales* ~

What if your merch isn't moving? We don't want to give our merchandise away, but neither do we want to be stuck with it. Putting a sale rack out or bins filled with clothing according to size (so clients don't have to search for pieces that will fit) are good ways to entice shoppers. Putting old pieces out at the start of the season is also a good way to get people's attention. We do a sale every year on Black Friday, the day after Thanksgiving, but we call it Fat Friday! This is a lighthearted way to encourage people to want to sweat and work off their indulgences from the day before. Be sure to state that the discounts are only on retail purchases so people know it's not applicable towards sessions and class packages. For example, you could offer $15 off a $100 purchase, $25 off a $150 purchase, $50 off a $250 purchase and $125 off $500.

You can also send out anniversary and birthday emails with a small incentive to boost retail sales:

To: ———
From: ———
Subject: ———

Dear Sandra,

It's your anniversary with Body Be Well Pilates! As our client you are very important to us and we greatly value your business. Please enjoy 25% off your next retail purchase AND one Private Session for $65.

As always, if you have any suggestions, comments, or requests about future sessions or classes, please let us know.

Hope to see you soon!

The Body Be Well Pilates Team

Bodybewell.com

To: ————
From: ————
Subject: ————

@

Dear Beth,

Body Be Well Pilates would like to wish you a very Happy Birthday! We all wish you health, love, wealth, happiness and, of course, plenty of cake! Please enjoy 25% off your next retail purchase with us!

We hope to see you soon.

The Body Be Well Pilates Team

Bodybewell.com

Having random flash day sales—"20% off any pair of leggings" or "25% off any top" can also help move product without you losing your shirt, financially speaking. You can be creative about promotions and flash sales based on your clients' interests, the location of your studio, and the seasons. Consider a buy-one-get-one sale, a post-winter sale, or a buy-more-get-more. For example:

- Buy 1 item and take 15% off!
- Buy 2 items and take 20% off
- Buy 3 items and take 30% off

## ~ *Events* ~

I mentioned hosting Thank You parties for your clients in the last chapter. Consider approaching your studio as an event space. Clients and their friends will start associating your studio with being fun and a great place to visit, even when they don't really need to shop or work out. Have you ever had people come to one of your parties who are not regular clients, just because?

You can create events around wellness and health, or just around fun, as a way to get people through your doors so you can show off your retail section. You'll likely sell some spandex, gain some new clients, and make your current clients feel great in the process!

Alternatively, you can offer to hold an event and/or teach a class in someone else's space. Here are a few concepts that worked for us:

- Sweat & Shop. We usually hold these events at night, and during the week. They start with a class and end with shopping, snacks and drinks—you can partner with a local juice bar and, if you're up for it, add alcohol too.

- Free Massage Day. Free massages can also attract customers—you'd be hard-pressed to find someone who *doesn't* want a free massage. Hire a massage therapist for the day and offer customers a bit of indulgence.

- Sip & Shop. Another nighttime event, the Sip and Shop is just about inviting clients to come by for some food and bubbly (Prosecco won't break the bank). These nights are super fun, make clients feel special and can be lucrative for you. They're just relaxing and fun evenings where people don't even have to work out. We usually have them on a Friday night and partner with some other local businesses. You can offer gift bags for the first 25 guests as an incentive to come early. Sip and Shops are a great opportunity for introducing new retail.

## ~ Invite Guest Retailers ~

Some of your clients might own a retail business or make things that they'd like to sell. Invite them to set up a table in your studio to introduce their products. We invited Derin International to come and sell their amazing Turkish towels and handmade soaps which complemented our retail. They also gave us items to include in our gift bags. Just make sure ahead of time that their product doesn't compete with any of yours. Even if you don't have a shop in your studio, inviting guest retailers is a fun way to create community. In that scenario, the retailer may give you an agreed-upon percentage of the day's proceeds.

## ~ Liquid Assets ~

Many breweries, wineries and even kombucha companies are interested in engaging with new markets, so keep them in mind as an addition to your events. They may draw in locals who will soon be your clients.

## ~ Food for Thought ~

Keep your mind and ears open. If you notice that your clients love food, offer a meal prep event with the help of a local restaurant, or a cooking demo with a local chef. If they want to learn more about nutrition, bring a nutritionist in who can answer their questions.

## ~ Give Back ~

We've found that our clients are motivated when events have a charitable component. You can team up with a local animal rescue or school supply drive. We have offered a Give Back Class with a suggested price to help raise money, and we've asked people to bring in school supplies to pay for their class. Don't forget to contribute as well, and maybe even have a product or two whose proceeds benefit a certain foundation.

Sometimes if we have merchandise that's been sitting around, we'll have a flash sale or give a small gift with purchase—grip socks, a canvas tote, a sample-size new product we love, or something branded with our logo.

### A Few More Tips For Moving Merch

- Keep Displays Fresh. Keep your clients guessing—a little, anyway. Every couple of weeks move displays around to prevent them from getting stale. And, of course, create new displays when new merchandise comes in.

- Tag Everything. You know how much you hate asking what something costs. Your clients do too, so make sure all your stock is priced.

- Talk Up the Products. We got amazing candles at the studio, with our logo on one side and a quote on the other. The scent was Champagne and they came packaged in a great bag. They sat on the desk and didn't budge. Then we made a sign explaining the company behind the candles, which is fair trade and generates meaningful income for the women artisans who make their products. These women are able to work from home while caring for their families, and they can use the extra income to send their children to school. Oftentimes these children will be the family's first generation of high school graduates.

Once we educated our clients about the company's background, we not only helped move the candles off the counter, we helped women artisans at the same time. That felt good all around.

### ~ Tags, Hangers and Bags, Oh My! ~

All the little extra bits required to sell retail add up! There are ways to make them pay for themselves—and then some.

Throwing away price tags or branded hang tags is wasting money. What if your tags had a purpose, just like every exercise? What if clients get 25% off their retail purchases for every five tags they save?

One of our clients saved her tags in a bowl, and when her friends came over for book club the bowl inspired a conversation. Some of those friends began coming to the studio and now they exercise and shop with us on a regular basis.

Bags can be pricey, but they're essential. And if you have a nice bag people will save it, reuse it and carry it around wherever they go. So brand yours with your logo and let it do some marketing for you. It makes my heart jump when I'm at the local farmers market or grocery store and I see our bags being reused. Yes they cost more than non-branded bags; however getting new clients is priceless!

# CHAPTER 11

# Don't Forget About You

---•---

*"Everyone is the architect of their own happiness."*
— Joseph Pilates

Your health is your business. If you don't take care of yourself, you can't take care of your clients, your family, or your team. This is why you need to create your "me time" and stick to it. Let's face it, if you don't schedule healthy into your life it does not happen.

How many of you have forgotten about YOU? For me this happens almost every year before Christmas. I go, go, go and then *wham*. I'm in bed for days, sleeping and snotting all over because I forgot to take care of myself. What the heck! I own a health-related business and teach Pilates and I'm the one down for the count. Anyone else guilty of this?

When I first opened my studio I was running full speed, working seven days a week to get it up and running, training all of my clients to be healthy and strong—and forgetting about my own workouts and fitness goals. I almost forgot what broccoli and kale looked like. Before I knew it, I had gained over 25 pounds and was so out of shape it wasn't even funny. I had become an unhealthy, angry chub-chub.

This rude awakening was a reminder in more ways than one that the most important thing we can do is take care of ourselves. Sometimes we just need to stop!

I know you might be thinking that you have a stressful job, an overly full schedule, and a busy family to take care of. You *have* to take care of everyone else first. I totally hear you, and I'm not trying to say it's easy and you should just eat some hummus and relax. We all have stress. It's a part of life. It comes and goes and comes and goes again. The trick is to deal with it when it comes, rather than letting it pile up.

Taking care of yourself is not selfish. It's the best thing you can do for everyone you care about. If you're not healthy, you can't help yourself and you surely can't help others. If you are only on point when you're not stressed and things are going smoothly, you aren't much good to yourself whenever a stress wave hits. Your life will be on a roller coaster of drama.

During a stop at the grocery store, I ran into a woman who hadn't been to the studio in months. At the fish counter we talked about the holidays and her kids and husband, how busy her life was and how she misses being at the studio and having time to exercise. She told me she felt selfish when she was at the studio and guilty for taking all that time for herself. I reminded her it was only two to three hours out of her 168-hour week! I also reminded her that a 50-minute workout is only 3.47% of her day.

I am in no way saying that we should stop caring for other people, but "me time" and our exercise time is so important. When I look at my own life, I know I have to plan ahead and make my exercise appointments or they won't happen. Some weeks I wake up on Monday and it seems that by nighttime it's Friday. Nothing got done, including my workouts.

As a studio owner and teacher, you have plenty of reasons to be a victim of burnout. I've been there, and I've seen it in my colleagues. We forget about ourselves. In order to keep teaching for a long time, we have to learn—right now—to take care of our own bodies so we can take care of our clients. It's one thing to take classes and train as a client, but quite different to be teaching.

Initially, it was very difficult for me to understand that I had to do less in order to keep doing more. While I was talking up the values of balance and a healthy lifestyle to my clients, I wasn't following my own advice. It took me a long time to overcome the dissatisfaction that had become my life, and it was only after taking the following steps that I "came back to myself" and started loving my job...and my life...again.

## ~ *Make You A Priority* ~

Make your me-time as important as the doctor's visit, the conference call, and your meeting with the contractor. Treat it just like any other appointment. For your mental, physical, and emotional well–being, you sometimes just need to stop. Then do something you *want* to do. Start with the simple stuff. Leave your phone somewhere and don't bring it with you to the dinner table. Read a magazine or book that has nothing to do with your profession. Get a massage or a pedicure. Let your family know you'll be making some time for yourself this month. Gradually, you'll notice that the email response can wait; the call doesn't have to be returned immediately and your family likes the way you look and act after your alone time.

## ~ *Make a Date with Your Workout* ~

Your exercise routine is just as important as the ones your clients enjoy. Schedule a workout outside the studio or gym. Go running, take a spin class, play tennis, hike, whatever...just make a commitment, like scheduling an appointment with a personal trainer, and get out of the studio and exercise. Not only will it keep you healthy, it will also remind you what it's like to be a client again—and you'll appreciate the energy being put into you, replacing what you give out all the time. Working out will also keep you from growing stale in your thinking—your clients will appreciate this too!

The gorgeous Lisa Hubbard, creator of *Rhythm Pilates*® says, "My health, fitness and well-being is one of my top three priorities, next to family and getting rest. I am in the habit of setting a schedule to work out with another instructor, take a group fitness class and/or yoga class about three times a week. The rest of the time I will work out on my own in my home studio or get outdoors. I find inspiration through an intention for the day and/or something new I might have learned. I typically film a video for social media after a class or during my own personal workout. It kills two birds with one stone."

## ~ *Enlist Your Clients* ~

Your clients are well equipped to change their own weights or springs and clean up after themselves. If you're not careful, you could find yourself bending over more than 100 times per shift, which is not a habit you want to get into. You may start feeling resentment towards your clients if you end up feeling physically poor—or if they're chronically late. So show them what their responsibilities are. It's likely that they'll be more than happy to help!

## ~ *Know Your Limit* ~

This is the hardest, but probably the most important thing you can do to avoid burnout. If we cut back on clients we automatically think we will be broke and unsuccessful. But, in the long run, by pacing yourself you'll make more money and have more energy. After my fifth client in a row, I start to go a little crazy! I want to give my sixth client as much energy as I gave to the five that came before, but realistically it's not going to happen. To keep up your stamina, plan breaks to eat and to re-energize. Take a quick 15-20 minute walk. Or eat something (most people get lunch breaks, you know) and you won't feel like snapping that 6$^{th}$ or 7$^{th}$ client in half like a twig. Don't schedule more than you can handle.

Nobody likes a grumpy teacher! Creating a healthy work–life balance is the key to maintaining a satisfying and successful career. Making yourself a priority enables you to generate energy, enthusiasm and passion for what you do. Don't feel guilty about taking time for yourself.

# CHAPTER 12

# Exercise Your Right to Exercise

————————————— • —————————————

*"Take care of your body. It's the only place you have to live."*
— Jim Rohn

After we make the commitment to put ourselves first what do we do?

We move!

Lack of time is one of the main reasons we avoid working out and put our fitness last. Below are some of my workouts (previously published on prevention.com), which you can fit in anytime and anywhere.

## The Quick Booty Workout You Can Do While You Wait For Your Coffee To Brew

Make those minutes count and perk up your butt with these simple toning exercises.

After a little bit of research (and a few cups of coffee), I found out it takes me about three minutes to fill and heat the water in my Keurig and about 30 seconds to fill my cup. So, of course, I had to come up with a quick workout to make those minutes really count!

Do this butt-sculpting workout in the a.m. or whenever you need a quick pick-me-up. Just by adding this short sequence to your routine you will gain more than 90 minutes of exercise a month and over 18 hours of movement a year—everything counts! Try to perform each move for 30-40 seconds or until your cup is brewed, and for best results, aim to flow from one movement to the next without stopping.

Feel free to use your counter for extra assistance or help balancing so you can focus on your form. Two hands are easiest, turning to the side and using one hand is a little harder, and no hands are most advanced. Pick what works for you.

If you're a newbie to butt workouts, you may not know how to activate your glutes. When you stand up or walk upstairs, you use your quads, but you don't use your glutes as much in everyday life. For this workout, really think about the muscles you're aiming to engage instead of just going through the motions—this way you will fire up those glutes!

## Plié Squat

1. Stand in a wide ballet second position with toes turned out, and hold onto your counter for support as needed.

2. Keeping your core pulled in and your shoulders back and down, bend your knees, making sure they track right over the middle of your foot.

3. Hold here for 30-40 seconds.

## Plié Squat with Heel Lifts

1. Just like in the above exercise, stay low in your wide and turned out plié.

2. Without bouncing your body up or down, peel your heels up and press through all 10 toes. Make sure to maintain your form and don't roll out or in with your ankles.

3. Perform 30-40 heel lifts, and try to deepen your squat a little bit, even towards the end when your legs are shaking.

## Plié Squat with Side Crunch

1. Still in the same wide second plié squat from above, press both heels into the floor and lace your hands behind your head with elbows out to the sides.

2. Keeping your core pulled in, bend to one side and squeeze your obliques in a side crunch. Come back up to center.

3. Repeat on the other side. Continue alternating for 30-40 reps total, making sure not to hinge forward or lose your core connection.

## Hamstring Press

1. Bring your legs into parallel and hip-distance apart, then bend both legs into a mini squat and maintain neutral with your core and pelvis.

2. Without arching into your lower back, lift one leg up into an "L" position and press it back behind you. Resist back to your start position without swinging.

3. Continue doing reps or, for an added challenge, hold the leg back and add little pulses for the 30-40 seconds of this interval. Don't forget to breathe!

## Bent Side Leg Lift

1. Staying in your mini squat from the above exercise, keep your legs parallel and your hips nice and level. Hover one leg off the floor in that bent "L" shape.

2. Holding your core in and your hip down, use your backside to lift one leg up to the side keeping the opposite leg stable and still.

3. Lower the raised leg back down, keeping your form and alignment, and repeat for 30-40 seconds.

## The One-Minute Magic Circle Workout That Will Trim And Tone Your Arms

Do these moves on the regular, and you will see results.

The magic circle is one of my favorite Pilates props. You can use it to tone your inner thighs and sculpt your core through small, controlled movements. Working my arms with the circle is also one of my favorite ways to strengthen them without using weights. Not only is it challenging, it's also a fun way to switch things up!

You can finish this sequence of arm exercises in just one minute, so you won't have any trouble finding time to do it 3-4 times a week. And trust me, you'll start to see and feel the results if you keep up with it. Try for 20 repetitions of each exercise below, and use control and resistance to really squeeze in on the circle. Stand up tall with your heels together and toes slightly turned out, and tweeze those inner thighs together the whole workout for some added burn!

### Overhead Tricep Presses (pictured on next page)

1. Bring the circle over your head holding onto the sides.

2. Bend your arms back overhead, then squeeze into the circle as you straighten the arms back up and overhead. Squeeze your triceps and the circle.

**Trainer Tip:** To work your arms even more in this exercise, do quick little pulses in on the circle while holding the arms behind the head.

Overhead Tricep Presses

### Side Single Arm Presses

1. Hold the circle at one hip, holding it in place with the hand on that same side.

2. Keep your elbow lifted and squeeze in on the circle, then resist back out. Make sure to do repetitions on both sides.

### Behind the Back Presses

1. Bring the circle behind you and hold onto the sides.

2. Squeeze into the circle trying to make it into an oval shape. These moves are hard, so know that it's okay if

the circle barely moves. Make sure to keep your shoulders down and away from your ears.

**Trainer Tip:** You can add little pulses to this move for an added exercise, if you like.

### ~ 4 Ways To Tone Your Inner Thighs With A Magic Circle ~

No matter how many times we squat, flex and squeeze our inner thighs together, it can seem like things just don't budge. That's when it's time to enlist a little bit of help. This workout uses a Pilates Magic Circle to fire up your inner thighs in new and different ways—which will lead to major toning and tightening. Perform each exercise for 20 seconds, and do the full routine 3 times.

### Tabletop Tweeze

1. Lying on your back, place the circle between your ankles, just above the joint, with the padded section touching your skin.
2. Curl your head, neck, and shoulders up and off the mat and look down at your core.
3. Gently resist in on the circle using your inner thighs and then, using just as much resistance, let the circle back out. Control the movement in both directions so that there's no bouncing. To make this even harder, elongate your legs and hold them at a 45-degree angle or lower.

### Standing Frog

1. Place the circle between your knees, right above the joint.

2. Glue your heels together, toes turned out in first position, and place your hands on your hips. Start to straighten your legs while squeezing the circle and keeping your heels glued together the whole time.

3. Bend the knees again and repeat for 20 seconds. Aim to take 3 seconds to bend and 3 seconds to straighten.

## Standing Fourth

1. Standing with one foot in front of the other, legs slightly turned out, place the circle between the ankles above the joint.

2. Keep your core pulled in while you shift your weight onto your back leg, all while holding the circle.

3. Start to squeeze the front leg toward the back leg, then switch sides and repeat. If turning out hurts your hips and joints, do this move with legs parallel.

## Standing Second

1. Bring your feet out to the sides in parallel and place the circle between your ankles, above the joints.

2. Keeping your balance, shift your weight over to one side while still holding the circle.

3. Squeeze the circle in and then control it back out. If you're having a hard time balancing, use a wall.

## ~ 4 *Super-Effective Inner Thigh Moves* ~

Getting into a workout routine can be intimidating when you're a beginner, especially if you don't know exactly which exercises you should do to tone your trouble spots. If you want to slim and strengthen your inner thighs, try starting with this simple circuit 2 or 3 times a week. Shoot for 8-10 repetitions of each move, and then progress to 12-15 reps, as you get stronger. Remember that it's okay to take breaks, and keep at it—consistency will lead you to see results in as little as 2 weeks if you're also sticking to a healthy diet.

## Frog

1. Lie on your back with your legs lifted into tabletop position and arms pushing into the mat at your sides. Join your heels together and turn your toes out at 45-degree angles.

2. With your core engaged, push your legs out long in front of you and just above the floor. The lower your legs are, the greater a challenge this will be for your abs. Keep inner thighs engaged by imagining that you are squeezing a $100 bill between your heels and don't want to drop it.

3. For a harder challenge, pulse your legs by bringing them halfway in and then back out. Lift your head, neck, and shoulders off the mat and look down at your core to feel the burn.

## Heel Pulse (pictured on next page)

1. Lie face down with your head resting gently on the backs of your hands.

2. Pull your core up and in toward your lower back, then slowly lift your legs about 2 inches. Think about how long you can extend rather than how high you can lift.

3. Turn your toes out and start to open and close your legs (about 6-8 inches), kicking your heels together and going as fast as you can without straining your lower back. Keep your legs straight the entire time, and squeeze your glutes.

Heel Pulse

## Lower Leg Lift

1. Lie on your side, lengthen your bottom leg, and cross the top leg over it. Rest your top foot either in front of or behind the bottom leg, depending on which feels better for your body. Prop your head up with your hand, or rest it on your arm.

2. Lift your bottom leg up, then lower it back down to hover just above the floor—but don't let it touch! Bring it right back up for another rep, and resist it back down again. Keep your torso still and pull in your abs to support your back.

3. Repeat on the other side.

Plié Pulses

1. Stand up and bring your feet out a little wider than hip-distance, with hips slightly externally rotated. Place your hands on your hips, out in front of you, or behind your head with elbows out to the sides.

2. Keeping your spine upright, bend your knees outward (for a ballerina-style plié) so they align over your ankles and don't roll in.

3. From your plié position, pull your core in and begin to pulse down and up without coming all the way to standing. See how low you can go without losing your form, and remember to breathe.

### ~ Jump Your Way To Weight Loss With This Quick Workout ~

These fun moves will also boost stability and bone strength to protect your joints.

Jumping can be scary. Sometimes the landing isn't pretty, and the "F" word comes to mind (no, not that one): Falling. But jumping can also be a terrific way to build stability and bone strength, and protect your joints.

These jumping exercises will definitely get your heart pumping. Rather than focus on how high you can get off the floor, though, pay attention to the control of your muscles through each movement. Smaller jumps are easier and larger jumps are harder, so listen to your body and do what is most safe and effective for you.

Side to Side

1. Stand with your legs hip-width apart and slightly bent.

2. Push using your legs and core to jump up and over to one side, as though you are jumping over something.

3. Land in starting position, and then continue to jump back and forth. Make sure to spring with your legs and roll through your foot to land. Aim for 10 jumps on each side.

Need a modification? Instead of jumping, just step side to side.

### Lunge to Lunge

1. First find your balance in lunge position, making sure to bend both the front knee and the back knee.

2. In one push, lift yourself up and off the ground.

3. Land the same way you started. Aim for 10 jumps on each side.

Lunge to Lunge

Need a modification? Do a mini-jump or skip jumping alto-
gether and just bend and straighten the legs.

## Lunge and Switch

1. These are similar to jumping jacks, but just in a different plane of movement. Start in your lunge with one
   leg front, one leg back, and both knees bent (just like
   the exercise above).

2. Jump up and switch legs, landing with the other leg in
   front. Melt through the knees and ankles.

3. Again try for 10 repetitions on each side, or 20
   switches. Remember to land softly and roll through
   the foot and bend the knees.

Need a modification? Rather than jump, lunge and then lift
your back foot up to your front knee height, then repeat on the
same side. For a greater challenge, lift the supporting heel and then
go back down.

## Inner Thigh Tweeze

1. Start in a wide squat position.

2. Push through both legs to jump into the air, all while
   holding your core in to protect your back.

3. Squeeze your inner thighs together, keeping the legs
   in parallel, and land back in your starting position. Try
   for 10 jumps.

Need a modification? Start in your squat and then shift your
weight over into one leg and lift the other leg up, squeezing your
inner thighs. Alternate to the other side, and try to keep your torso
upright as you switch. With this variation, do 5 lifts on each side.

## ~ *Pilates Exercises To Ease And Prevent Back Pain* ~

Nagging back pain can come at any age, and all too many of us are familiar with it. According to the American Chiropractic Association, half of all working Americans report feeling back pain every year, and as a nation, we spend at least $50 billion annually to find relief. Ouch.

The good thing is, most back pain isn't caused by a serious medical condition, but rather everyday habits like poor posture, exercise, or simply sitting too much. By strengthening the core and releasing tension and tightness around the upper and lower back, you can usually ease the pain—and even prevent it.

The Pilates exercises below will connect you to your deep core muscles so they can support your back and remove strain there. To really feel a difference, do this routine twice a week consistently. Do note that it's best to consult a doctor and get to the root of your back pain before starting a program like this on your own. Remember to go slowly and gently, and always listen to your body—you should never do anything that hurts!

### Pelvic Bridge

This exercise strengthens the low back, as well as the quads, glutes, hamstrings, and abs. It's essential that you engage your abs in this position to avoid sagging into the low back and straining it.

1. Lie on your back with knees bent and feet positioned about a hand's distance from your butt. Keep your arms long at your sides with palms flat on the floor.

2. Press through the entire area of your feet, squeeze your backside, and lift your hips off the floor until your shoulders, hips, and knees are in a straight line. Relax your upper body and make sure you don't roll into your neck. Hold in this position for a slow count of 10.

3. Inhale as you slowly lower your body back to start position, remembering to keep your core engaged. Perform 2 or 3 sets of 10-12 repetitions.

## Half Chest Curl

Rather than do full sit-ups, which can aggravate your low back if you're experiencing pain there, strengthen your abs in this half chest curl that also works your back muscles.

1. Lie with knees bent and feet flat on the floor. Cross arms over your chest or put hands behind your neck for support. Proper form prevents excessive stress on your low back, so make sure your feet, tailbone, and lower back remain in contact with the mat as you continue through this move.

2. Tighten your abs and peel your shoulders off the floor, breathing out as you raise your shoulders even higher. Try to work from your core, and don't lead with your elbows or pull on your neck. Hold here for a second, and then slowly lower back down. Repeat 8-10 times.

## Forearm Plank

If you only have time for one pose, this is the ultimate core move. It really works the entire midsection, including the deep core muscles and the back, as well as the waist, hips, legs, buttocks, arms, and shoulders.

1. Lie on your mat and place your elbows directly under your shoulders. Tuck under your toes and press firmly through the backs of your legs and heels.

2. Engage your lower abs and tighten your core as you lift your body up off the floor and come into a straight line from head to toe. Don't let your ribs splay open or

Forearm Plank

your butt sag or lift too high. Hold for 30-60 seconds, and then lower down. Repeat 2 or 3 more times.

## Child's Pose

This restful stretch is a nice way to end a low back series because it helps align the spine and release tension in the low back.

1. Start on hands and knees, and then bring your hips back to sit toward your heels as much as possible. If you need more of a lower back stretch, keep knees closer together; if you need more of a hip stretch, take knees farther apart.

2. Stretch your arms out in front of you with palms resting on the floor. Relax your forehead to the ground, and breathe deeply.

3. To come out, crawl your hands toward your legs and slowly sit up. Let the head be the last to come up. Repeat and hold again for as long as needed.

### ~ 4 Ways To Build Stronger Bones With Pilates ~

When was the last time you said to yourself, "I will go to the gym today and work out my bones?" Too often we focus on the number on a scale or fitting into a pair of pants from over a decade ago, rather than improving our overall health. But our bones are our support systems, and they're pretty darn important.

This workout will strengthen your bones with gentle Pilates-based exercises. Weight training and balancing moves stress the body and stimulate bone cells, in turn making your bones stronger and denser. Through functional movement and muscle strengthening, you can also improve your balance and ward off injuries. Add this sequence to your weekly exercise routine—which should also include at least 30 minutes of aerobic exercise, five days a week, according to American Bone Health—to build bone strength and prevent osteoporosis down the road.

## Standing Hip Abduction

1. From standing, pitch your body slightly forward, place hands on your hips, and bend your knees slightly. Bring one leg out to the side so your weight is in the other leg. Feel free to hold onto a stable chair or wall if you need help balancing.

2. Carefully lift your extended leg off the ground, keeping it straight and maintaining your form by pulling in your core.

3. Lower your raised foot to the floor and repeat 8-10 times. Switch to the other side for 8-10 more reps.

## Standing Hip Extension

1. Standing with your hips squared under your shoulders and knees slightly bent, pitch forward and lift one leg

behind you. Feel free to hold onto a chair or wall if you need help balancing.

2. Carefully lift your raised leg even higher without hiking your hips—this requires a stable core.

3. Lower the foot to the floor and repeat 8-10 times. Switch to the other leg for 8-10 reps on that side.

### Modified Single Leg Stretch

1. Lying on your back with your head, neck, and shoulders down, pull one knee in towards your shoulder. Reach the other leg out long to 45 degrees using strength from your core. Make sure to keep your head down so there is no flexion of the spine.

2. Alternate legs. Repeat 8-10 times on each leg, and really push those hands into your bent knee to create resistance.

### Swimming

1. Lying face down; stretch your arms out long in front of you and your legs out back behind you.

2. Lift your arms and legs off the ground an inch or two, and keep your gaze downward so you don't crunch your neck.

3. Breathing normally, start to kick your arms and legs up and down as quickly as you can for 8-10 seconds.

### ~If You Hate Running, This Is The Perfect Fat-Burning Cardio Workout For You~

You can do it anywhere—no experience necessary.

Cardio workouts can be intimidating—especially if you're overweight or trying to get into shape. That's where this workout comes in. It's the perfect way to ease into fat-burning cardio without injuring yourself.

With this circuit, you will be able to go at your own tempo and speed. As you get stronger, feel free to up your speed to increase your heart rate even more. These movements are not huge, so they should be pretty easy on your joints. But always listen to your body and remember this workout is about you and not a competition with anyone else!

Start by doing this workout just two times a week, and then increase to three or four times a week as you build stamina. Try for 20 repetitions of each exercise, and for the moves that switch sides, do 20 on each side.

### Squat/Star Jump

1. Start in a wide second squat position with your feet wide, toes turned slightly out. Place your hands on your thighs or clasp them in front of your chest.

2. Push with your legs and through your core to jump up and out into a "star" position.

3. Return to your start position, making sure that you roll through your foot to land.

### Plank Jacks

1. Start in a strong plank position with your legs glued together. If you need to go onto your forearms, you can do that, too!

2. Jump your legs out to the sides and then back together, making sure your backside isn't going up and down as you do so. Use control and keep your core in to protect your back.

### Lunge Kick Backs

1. Start in a deep lunge position with hands on your hips.

2. Push into your front leg and lift your back leg out behind you. There is a balance challenge here, so if needed, keep one hand on something stable.

3. Bring the back leg down to the floor and back into your starting position.

Plié Hops

### Plié Hops (pictured on previous page)

1. Come into a wide second position with your arms out in front you. Bend into a plié, keeping your knees directly over the middle of your feet.

2. Push with your legs and through your core to hop up, and then gently land back in starting position.

### Rolling Like a Ball to Standing

1. Start on the ground in a ball position. Keeping this shape, roll back to the top of your shoulders.

2. Use your core to come back up to your start position, and let your feet find the floor.

3. Push through those legs to bring yourself up to standing. Add a mini hop if you can before going back down to roll through another rep

Rolling Like a Ball to Standing

# CHAPTER 13
# The To-Don't List

———————— • ————————

*"The difference between successful people and really successful people is that really successful people say no to almost everything."*
— Warren Buffett

I'm a list maker. Always have been. I like lists because they make me feel like I'm moving forward (or at least trying to), and because checking things off feels great. But how often do we actually complete our entire To-Do list? I usually get so overwhelmed by mine that I end up spending two or three hours looking at complete strangers and adorable puppy videos on social media and getting nothing done! If this sounds like you, it may be time for a To-Don't list.

I've found that, unlike a To-Do list, which has a way of making me anxious or even break out into hives, a To-Don't list keeps me sane (and hive-free). The To-Don't list is a list of things you want to constantly focus on not doing and it will free up your schedule—so you can focus on the things that really matter without getting lost on those that don't move you forward.

The To-Don't list is going to be around for a while and you'll want to keep referring back to it. You can't accomplish the items once, check them off, crumple the list and throw it out. You have to start developing your To-Don't list as a habit. This can also be exhausting, but it's super beneficial in the long run. There are only so many hours in the day and there's no sense wasting them on things that don't matter.

I know, I can hear you saying that your studio or situation is different and you have dozens of important things you *must* do. But the truth is, not everything is equally important and you are the one who can best decide how to spend your time.

Keep your list short so you don't get overwhelmed. Here's a sample of mine:

*Don't schedule meetings with everyone who asks.*

There were times when I rearranged my schedule (I even moved clients' sessions around) to have a meeting with someone I didn't even know. I had no clue what the meeting was supposed to accomplish, I didn't know the goal or purpose and there was no plan or resolution at the end. No more. I only schedule meetings when I am 100% sure that it will be productive and help move me forward.

*Don't do stuff you hate.*

Whether it's training a certain client, attending a useless networking event or eating beets! Just stop it. Stop wasting your time and energy.

*Don't wait for the perfect time.*

This includes making time for you. Let's face it there's often going to be something in the way of what you want or need to do—someone coming to visit, your kids lacrosse schedule, work, the weather, money, your mother or mother-in-law, your goldfish, etc. Whatever it is, you can always find a reason for it "not being the right time" to do something. Do it anyway.

Once you have your To-Don't list ready, keep it in a place where you can see it throughout the day. Each morning, think about what you want to accomplish and remind yourself of what you will NOT be doing. You can always add new things to your list as you become more aware of how you spend your time.

You can also use your To-Don't list as a way to set stronger boundaries for yourself and your business. Saying No to certain things makes the things you choose to say Yes to that much more clear and powerful.

Remember, giving up and saying No are two very different things. When things aren't adding up in your life, it's time to start subtracting. You will be surprised at how much more you can get done in less time, while growing your business and having a life.

Useless worry is one of the things on my To-Don't list. Over the years of owning my studios I have received many emails that, at the time, really upset me. Now they crack me up and remind me of how much the business has evolved. Even when they were hurtful, I knew the emails were just too good to throw out, so I printed them and saved them in a box. Sometimes I go through them when I need a laugh and to help remind myself that I am doing okay. Enjoy!

Dearest Chelsea,

Your studio is so great! I love all your classes and everything about your place except one thing...the toilet paper. I know you are a new business owner and slammed with so many other more important things so I don't mean to bother you with this, but your toilet paper pills and gets stuck. I don't want you to worry about it so I have decided to bring my own toilet paper and lock it up so I can use it when I am at the studio every week. I hope you have a nice week.

Fondly,

Insane (Ex) Client

Hello!

I would like to make an appointment to try private sessions at your studio. I have a gift card from a different Pilates studio that I would like to use for payment. I figured since Pilates is just Pilates this will be fine. Please let me know what you have available for me.

Thank you,

Not Happening for You Client

Dear Chelsea,

I have been taking classes at your studio for a few years now and I notice that some of your teachers don't always get to a person in time to correct their form while doing the exercises. I thought that because I have been taking so long that you wouldn't mind if I correct other students in my classes to help everyone out. Let me know what you think!

Thanks,

Are You Out of Your Mind Client

Hi Chelsea,

I hope you're having an amazing week! I just wanted to suggest a few things for you to make my time at your studio better for myself and everyone else:

1. Get a different brand of water because the one that you have tastes bad.

2. More color options for socks since all the dark colors available are depressing.

3. Select-a-size paper towels so there isn't so much waste and trash in your garbage.

4. A class just on arms because I know myself and other women just like to work their arms.

5. And finally if each reformer could get their own individualized fan by it so I wouldn't sweat so much and could have a breeze on me while working out that would be great too.

Looking forward to seeing some changes,

Not Happening Lady Client

# CHAPTER 14

# Remembering Why We Are Teachers

├─────────────── • ─────────────┤

*"In learning you will teach, and in teaching you will learn."*
— Phil Collins

With all the extraneous things we do to keep our business vibrant and viable—is it time to paint the studio, retile the bathroom, pay our landlord and/or the IRS, restock the toilet paper inventory? —it's easy to forget what got us here in the first place. Teaching.

I can still remember my very first week at our Catskill studio. Sarah suffered from frequent back pain, tight hips, rounded shoulders, sore wrists, and sometimes pain/numbness that would start in the legs and end up at her feet. She wanted more than anything to drop 30 pounds and fix her back pain and be healthy again. Sound familiar?

After our initial conversations about her body and goals, we performed several different muscular strength, flexibility, and coordination exercises, and ended with balance work. After the session, we discussed her strengths and weaknesses and what I thought would be an appropriate program for her body. Sarah seemed satisfied, but for whatever reason didn't want to commit to personal training sessions. She told me her routine at the gym was working for her and that she would start to implement my homework exercises to help with her back and other pain. Then Sarah disappeared.

Six months later she reappeared at the studio for another private session. She told me that she hadn't gotten anywhere and decided to start one-on-one sessions with me. Within a few months, her back pain had disappeared completely, she felt taller, and had lost nine inches from her waist! Her only regret, she told me, was not committing and starting six months before. Sarah is just one example of someone whose progress reminds me of why I became a teacher in the first place, and why I wanted to open a studio.

She's also an ideal example of someone who benefited from one-on-one training, which gives clients the opportunity to deal with their specific body issues.

In a perfect world, everyone new to a fitness regime would stick to beginner classes or take private lessons before jumping into more advanced group classes. But we all know that doesn't always happen! Instead, we might find ourselves teaching a class which has one person who has never done Pilates, yoga or whatever it is that's your specialty, one client who has been a regular for over five years, one recovering from a shoulder injury and two with serious disc and back issues. Now what? (It might be too early to have wine.)

What do we do when new clients only take one initial private session (if we're lucky) and then think they're ready for group classes? What do we do when people jump into the "wrong" class? How do we manage our group classes without getting frustrated, or worse, having our clients get hurt?

I have come up with four tips that you may want to use to help you teach a better group class in which you and your clients should all be able to enjoy the journey, work hard and have fun!

How are your bodies today?

It's nice to ask everyone how they're feeling before class, even though we're probably familiar with our regular clients' bodies. This gives everyone, including anyone new, an opportunity to speak up. This also gives our regulars a chance to let us know if they overdid it with the grandkids on the weekend, played too much tennis or didn't get enough sleep. It also gives you a heads-up on how you might have to modify or vary certain exercises for the safety of your clients, and helps bridge the gap between you and the class. By establishing your attentiveness and professionalism, you let them know that you care.

Compliment vs. Correction!

When teaching a group, there may be many different levels and personalities. Some will appreciate corrections while some may take them as criticism. Aim for balance. Get to know your clients. If you know someone might feel embarrassed if you call them out, maybe pull them aside after the class and take a minute to explain how they can make a certain exercise better for their bodies. Instead of using names in class maybe just use a general cue in hopes that the person with their shoulders up to their ears hears you and pulls them back and down. Or just go over to the client and quietly give hands-on help to get them where you want them to be. Be ready to quickly swap a correction for a compliment or vice versa.

We want all of our clients to feel motivated and inspired to do the exercises properly and not to be embarrassed if they can't seem to get it right. If you notice a client just can't do Stomach Massage, but is rocking Climb a Tree, you could say something like: "Your Climb a Tree is awesome and your hamstrings have gotten so much stronger. Now let's work on making that Stomach Massage just as fabulous!" Not only did you prevent your client from receiving the Worst Stomach Massage Form in the World award, you created an even deeper rapport, thus strengthening your relationship.

Breathe and Get a "Check-In"!

Our clients work so hard, yet sometimes when we give them a challenge their form and alignment just aren't cutting it. One thing we offer at our studios is a "Check-In Session" once a month. Any of our clients who take group classes are offered one discounted private per month. We also let them use three of their already purchased group class packages to pay for their private. This way it's already paid for and they can schedule a private session where we can work with them on exactly what they need.

The "Check-In Sessions" have been very beneficial because they help clients get used to new exercises and the "language" of the movement. They also show the clients how nice it is to get 100% of the instructor's time. A lot of "groupies" have even started buying small packs of privates and fitting them in more than once a month.

Remember your first time!

It's very easy for us to forget what it's like from the student or client's point of view, which is why I highly recommend that trainers work with a trainer of their own and take classes on a regular basis. Not only does this help them understand their clients' experience, it also keeps them on their game physically.

Taking classes can be a great reminder of what it requires to create an exceptional experience for our clients. I find that these classes bring me back into my client's perspective and help me feel what they feel, see what they see, and hear what they hear.

Remember that not everyone *loves* exercising. In fact, most clients are intimidated to be in a class, so lighten the mood and add your personality and maybe a little humor to make a comforting and welcoming atmosphere. Working out and teaching are supposed to be fun.

# In the End

———————————— • ————————————

Owning and running a studio can be more rewarding than you can imagine. As I've said before, there's no single approach that works for everyone—and at some point, trust me, you'll mess up. A decade later, I'm still asking myself, Am I doing this right?

But being "right" sometimes means being too careful. At the end of the day you want a kitchen sink full of dishes, maybe some empty wine bottles and flour spread over the counter from making pizzas and memories. I'm still learning as I go, making mistakes and occasionally doubting myself, but what I've discovered about entrepreneurship is that it is okay to be uncomfortable. Being uncomfortable is, in my opinion, one of the keys to longevity as an entrepreneur. It keeps you on your toes, ready to adapt. Complacency is a killer.

I can't tell you whether opening a studio is the right thing for you, but if you feel an uncontrollable urge to go out and create something in the world, take that desire seriously. Be aggressive about learning as much as you can about how to make your dream a successful reality.

The best things take effort and hard work. Keep going and

plow through until you reach your goal. Then you can take a breath and say, "Well that wasn't easy, but look what I've done!"

Opening and running a studio requires stamina and single-mindedness, but allows you to be endlessly creative—let the business reflect your personality. You can be super ambitious *and* super fun. You can care deeply about your business *and* love Champagne, sequins, and sneakers, all at the same time. I loved watching my studios go from an idea to a reality, and now I love running them. I hope the advice I've given will help you create the studio of your dreams, and that you have as much fun with your business as I continue to have with mine.

# About the Author

———————————————— • ————————————————

Chelsea Streifeneder is a recognized Pilates Method Alliance® Certified Teacher, Pilatespreneur, speaker, writer, and the proud owner of Body Be Well Pilates studios in Red Hook and Catskill, NY. She began her career as a Pilates teacher in Los Angeles after graduating from Bard College with a B.A. in Writing and Dance.

Streifeneder has been featured on *Coffee with America, Pilates Unfiltered,* and as one of Dutchess County's Forty Under 40 Mover & Shaker Honorees. Her own articles and workouts have been featured in *Prevention, Women's Health, AARP, Hudson Valley Magazine,* and she has appeared on the cover of *Pilates Style Magazine.* Streifeneder channels her love of Pilates, fitness and health into helping others make their bodies and businesses healthy and strong.

If you have any Pilates or fitness-related questions Chelsea would be more than happy to address them! For professional speaking engagements, seminars or workshops, please email: chelsea@bodybewellpilates.com.

You can also find her on Facebook at facebook.com/chelsea.streifeneder

and on Instagram

@chelseastreifeneder.

Please visit her website, bodybewellpilates.com, for additional information.

# Morgan James
# Speakers Group

We connect Morgan James published authors with live and online events and audiences who will benefit from their expertise.

 Morgan James makes all of our titles available
through the Library for All Charity Organization.

www.LibraryForAll.org

CPSIA information can be obtained
at www.ICGtesting.com
Printed in the USA
BVHW030145120119
537698BV00001B/9/P

9 781642 790603